First World War
and Army of Occupation
War Diary
France, Belgium and Germany

15 DIVISION
Divisional Troops
Royal Army Medical Corps
Divisional Field Ambulance Workshop Unit
9 July 1915 - 31 March 1916

WO95/1932/3

The Naval & Military Press Ltd
www.nmarchive.com
Published in association with The National Archives

Published by

The Naval & Military Press Ltd

Unit 10 Ridgewood Industrial Park,

Uckfield, East Sussex,

TN22 5QE England

Tel: +44 (0) 1825 749494

www.naval-military-press.com

www.nmarchive.com

This diary has been reprinted in facsimile from the original. Any imperfections are inevitably reproduced and the quality may fall short of modern type and cartographic standards.

© **Crown Copyright**
Images reproduced by permission of The National Archives, London, England, 2015.

Contents

Document type	Place/Title	Date From	Date To
Heading	WO95/1932/3		
Heading	15th Division 15th Fld Amb Workshop Unit. Jly 1915-Mar 1916		
Heading	15th Division 15th Ambulance Workshop Unit Vol I 9-31-7-15		
Heading	War Diary 15th Divnl Field Ambulance Workshop Unit. From July 9th 1915-July 31st 1915.		
War Diary		09/07/1915	31/07/1915
Heading	15th Division 15th Divl. F.a. Workshop Unit Vol II August 15		
War Diary	Hesdigneul	10/08/1915	15/08/1915
War Diary	Vaudricourt	15/08/1915	15/08/1915
War Diary	Noeux-Les-Mines	15/08/1915	15/08/1915
War Diary	Hesdigneul	16/08/1915	16/08/1915
War Diary	Vaudricourt.	16/08/1915	16/08/1915
War Diary	Noeux-Les-Mines	16/08/1915	16/08/1915
War Diary	Hesdigneul	17/08/1915	17/08/1915
War Diary	Vaudricourt	17/08/1915	17/08/1915
War Diary	Noeux-Les-Mines	17/08/1915	17/08/1915
War Diary	Hesdigneul	18/08/1915	18/08/1915
War Diary	Vaudricourt.	18/08/1915	18/08/1915
War Diary	Noeux-Les-Mines.		
War Diary	Hesdigneul	19/08/1915	19/08/1915
War Diary	Vaudricourt.	19/08/1915	19/08/1915
War Diary	Noeux-Les-Mines.	19/08/1915	19/08/1915
War Diary	Hesdigneul	19/08/1915	20/08/1915
War Diary	Vaudricourt	20/08/1915	20/08/1915
War Diary	Noeux-Les-Mines.	20/08/1915	20/08/1915
War Diary	Hesdigneul	20/08/1915	21/08/1915
War Diary	Vaudricourt	21/08/1915	21/08/1915
War Diary	Noeux-Les-Mines.	21/08/1915	21/08/1915
War Diary	Hesdigneul	22/08/1915	22/08/1915
War Diary	Vaudricourt	22/08/1915	22/08/1915
War Diary	Noeux-Les-Mines.	22/08/1915	22/08/1915
War Diary	Hesdigneul	23/08/1915	23/08/1915
War Diary	Vaudricourt.	23/08/1915	23/08/1915
War Diary	Hesdigneul	24/08/1915	24/08/1915
War Diary	Vaudricourt.	24/08/1915	24/08/1915
War Diary	Noeux-Les-Mines.	24/08/1915	24/08/1915
War Diary	Hesdigneul	25/08/1915	25/08/1915
War Diary	Vaudricourt	25/08/1915	25/08/1915
War Diary	Noeux-Les-Mines.		
War Diary	Hesdigneul.	26/08/1915	26/08/1915
War Diary	Hesdigneul & Labeuvriere	26/08/1915	26/08/1915
War Diary	Vaudricourt	26/08/1915	26/08/1915
War Diary	Hesdigneul	27/08/1915	27/08/1915
War Diary	Labeuvriere	27/08/1915	27/08/1915
War Diary	Vaudricourt.	27/08/1915	27/08/1915
War Diary	Noeux-Les-Mines	27/08/1915	27/08/1915
War Diary	Hesdigneul	28/08/1915	28/08/1915

War Diary	La Beuvriere	28/08/1915	28/08/1915
War Diary	Vaudricourt.	28/08/1915	28/08/1915
War Diary	Noeux-Les-Mines.	28/08/1915	28/08/1915
War Diary	Hesdigneul	29/08/1915	29/08/1915
War Diary	Labeuvriere	29/08/1915	29/08/1915
War Diary	Vaudricourt.	29/08/1915	29/08/1915
War Diary	Noeux-Les-Mines.	29/08/1915	29/08/1915
War Diary	Hesdigneul	30/08/1915	30/08/1915
War Diary	Labeuvriere	30/08/1915	30/08/1915
War Diary	Vaudricourt.	30/08/1915	30/08/1915
War Diary	Noeux-Les-Mines.	30/08/1915	30/08/1915
War Diary	Hesdigneul	31/08/1915	31/08/1915
War Diary	Labeuvriere	31/08/1915	31/08/1915
War Diary	Vaudricourt.	31/08/1915	31/08/1915
War Diary	Noeux-Les-Mines.	31/08/1915	31/08/1915
War Diary		01/08/1915	09/08/1915
Heading	15th Division 15th Divl. F.A. W.U. Vol 3 Sept. 15		
War Diary	Hesdigneul	01/09/1915	01/09/1915
War Diary	Labeuvriere	01/09/1915	01/09/1915
War Diary	Vaudricourt	01/09/1915	01/09/1915
War Diary	Noeux-Les-Mines.	01/09/1915	01/09/1915
War Diary	Hesdigneul	02/09/1915	02/09/1915
War Diary	Labeuvriere.	02/09/1915	02/09/1915
War Diary	Vaudricourt.	02/09/1915	02/09/1915
War Diary	Noeux-Les-Mines	02/09/1915	02/09/1915
War Diary	Hesdigneul	03/09/1915	03/09/1915
War Diary	Labeuvriere	03/09/1915	03/09/1915
War Diary	Noeux-Les-Mines.	03/09/1915	03/09/1915
War Diary	Hesdigneul	04/09/1915	04/09/1915
War Diary	Labeuvriere	04/09/1915	04/09/1915
War Diary	Vaudricourt.	04/09/1915	04/09/1915
War Diary	Noeux-Les-Mines.	04/09/1915	04/09/1915
War Diary	Hesdigneul	05/09/1915	05/09/1915
War Diary	Labeuvriere & Noeux-Les-Mines.	05/09/1915	05/09/1915
War Diary	Vaudricourt.	05/09/1915	05/09/1915
War Diary	Noeux-Les-Mines.	05/09/1915	05/09/1915
War Diary	Hesdigneul.	06/09/1915	06/09/1915
War Diary	Noeux-Les-Mines.	06/09/1915	06/09/1915
War Diary	Labeuvriere.	06/09/1915	06/09/1915
War Diary	Vaudricourt.	06/09/1915	06/09/1915
War Diary	Noeux-Les-Mines.	06/09/1915	06/09/1915
War Diary	Hesdigneul.	07/09/1915	07/09/1915
War Diary	Labeuvriere	07/09/1915	07/09/1915
War Diary	Vaudricourt.	07/09/1915	07/09/1915
War Diary	Noeux-Les-Mines.	07/09/1915	07/09/1915
War Diary	Hesdigneul	08/09/1915	08/09/1915
War Diary	Labeuvriere.	08/09/1915	08/09/1915
War Diary	Vaudricourt	08/09/1915	08/09/1915
War Diary	Noeux-Les-Mines.	08/09/1915	08/09/1915
War Diary	Hesdigneul	09/09/1915	09/09/1915
War Diary	Labeuvriere	09/09/1915	09/09/1915
War Diary	Noeux-Les-Mines.	09/09/1915	09/09/1915
War Diary	Vaudricourt.	09/09/1915	09/09/1915
War Diary	Noeux-Les-Mines.	09/09/1915	09/09/1915
War Diary	Hesdigneul	10/09/1915	10/09/1915
War Diary	Labeuvriere	10/09/1915	10/09/1915

War Diary	Noeux-Les-Mines.	10/09/1915	10/09/1915
War Diary	Vaudricourt	10/09/1915	10/09/1915
War Diary	Noeux-Les-Mines.	10/09/1915	10/09/1915
War Diary	Hesdigneul.	11/09/1915	11/09/1915
War Diary	Labeuvriere	11/09/1915	11/09/1915
War Diary	Vaudricourt.	11/09/1915	11/09/1915
War Diary	Noeux-Les-Mines.	11/09/1915	11/09/1915
War Diary	Hesdigneul	12/09/1915	12/09/1915
War Diary	Labeuvriere.	12/09/1915	12/09/1915
War Diary	Noeux-Les-Mines.	12/09/1915	12/09/1915
War Diary	Vaudricourt.	12/09/1915	12/09/1915
War Diary	Noeux-Les-Mines.	12/09/1915	12/09/1915
War Diary	Hesdigneul.	13/09/1915	13/09/1915
War Diary	Labeuvriere.	13/09/1915	13/09/1915
War Diary	Vaudricourt.	13/09/1915	13/09/1915
War Diary	Noeux-Les-Mines.	13/09/1915	13/09/1915
War Diary	Hesdigneul	14/09/1915	14/09/1915
War Diary	Labeuvriere & Noeux-Les-Mines.	14/09/1915	14/09/1915
War Diary	Vaudricourt	14/09/1915	14/09/1915
War Diary	Noeux-Les-Mines.	14/09/1915	14/09/1915
War Diary	Hesdigneul	15/09/1915	15/09/1915
War Diary	Labeuvriere	15/09/1915	15/09/1915
War Diary	Noeux-Les-Mines.	15/09/1915	15/09/1915
War Diary	Vaudricourt	15/09/1915	15/09/1915
War Diary	Vaudricourt.	15/09/1915	15/09/1915
War Diary	Hesdigneul	16/09/1915	16/09/1915
War Diary	Labeuvriere	16/09/1915	16/09/1915
War Diary	Noeux-Les-Mines.	16/09/1915	16/09/1915
War Diary	Vaudricourt.	16/09/1915	16/09/1915
War Diary	Noeux-Les-Mines.	16/09/1915	16/09/1915
War Diary	Hesdigneul	17/09/1915	17/09/1915
War Diary	Labeuvriere	17/09/1915	17/09/1915
War Diary	Noeux-Les-Mines.	17/09/1915	17/09/1915
War Diary	Vaudricourt.	17/09/1915	17/09/1915
War Diary	Noeux-Les-Mines.	17/09/1915	17/09/1915
War Diary	Hesdigneul.	18/09/1915	18/09/1915
War Diary	Labeuvriere	18/09/1915	18/09/1915
War Diary	Noeux-Les-Mines.	18/09/1915	18/09/1915
War Diary	Vaudricourt.	18/09/1915	18/09/1915
War Diary	Noeux-Les-Mines.	18/09/1915	18/09/1915
War Diary	Hesdigneul	19/09/1915	19/09/1915
War Diary	Labeuvriere	19/09/1915	19/09/1915
War Diary	Noeux-Les-Mines.	19/09/1915	19/09/1915
War Diary	Vaudricourt	19/09/1915	19/09/1915
War Diary	Noeux-Les-Mines.	19/09/1915	19/09/1915
War Diary	Hesdigneul	20/09/1915	20/09/1915
War Diary	Noeux-Les-Mines.	20/09/1915	20/09/1915
War Diary	Labeuvriere.	20/09/1915	20/09/1915
War Diary	Vaudricourt	20/09/1915	20/09/1915
War Diary	Noeux-Les-Mines.	20/09/1915	20/09/1915
War Diary	Hesdigneul	21/09/1915	21/09/1915
War Diary	Noeux-Les-Mines.	21/09/1915	21/09/1915
War Diary	Labeuvriere.	21/09/1915	21/09/1915
War Diary	Vaudricourt.	21/09/1915	21/09/1915
War Diary	Noeux-Les-Mines.	21/09/1915	21/09/1915
War Diary	Hesdigneul.	22/09/1915	22/09/1915

War Diary	Noeux-Les-Mines.	22/09/1915	22/09/1915
War Diary	Mazingarbe.	22/09/1915	22/09/1915
War Diary	Labeuvriere.	22/09/1915	22/09/1915
War Diary	Vaudricourt.	22/09/1915	22/09/1915
War Diary	Noeux-Les-Mines.	22/09/1915	22/09/1915
War Diary	Hesdigneul.	23/09/1915	23/09/1915
War Diary	Noeux-Les-Mines. & Labeuvriere.	23/09/1915	23/09/1915
War Diary	Vaudricourt.	23/09/1915	23/09/1915
War Diary	Noeux-Les-Mines.	23/09/1915	23/09/1915
War Diary	Hesdigneul.	24/09/1915	24/09/1915
War Diary	Mazingarbe.	24/09/1915	24/09/1915
War Diary	Noeux-Les-Mines.	24/09/1915	24/09/1915
War Diary	Vaudricourt	24/09/1915	24/09/1915
War Diary	Noeux-Les-Mines.	24/09/1915	24/09/1915
War Diary	Hesdigneul.	25/09/1915	25/09/1915
War Diary	Noeux-Les-Mines.	25/09/1915	25/09/1915
War Diary	Hesdigneul.	26/09/1915	27/09/1915
War Diary	Noeux-Les-Mines.	27/09/1915	27/09/1915
War Diary	Vaudricourt	27/09/1915	27/09/1915
War Diary	Noeux-Les-Mines.	27/09/1915	27/09/1915
War Diary	Hesdigneul.	28/09/1915	28/09/1915
War Diary	Noeux-Les-Mines.	28/09/1915	28/09/1915
War Diary	Vaudricourt.	28/09/1915	28/09/1915
War Diary	Hesdigneul	29/09/1915	29/09/1915
War Diary	Noeux-Les-Mines.	29/09/1915	29/09/1915
War Diary	Vaudricourt.	29/09/1915	29/09/1915
War Diary	Noeux-Les-Mines.	29/09/1915	29/09/1915
War Diary	Hesdigneul.	30/09/1915	30/09/1915
War Diary	Vaudricourt.	30/09/1915	30/09/1915
War Diary	Noeux-Les-Mines.	30/09/1915	30/09/1915
Heading	15th Division 15th Divl. F.A.W.U. Vol 4 Oct 15		
War Diary	Labuissiere	01/10/1915	01/10/1915
War Diary	Vaudricourt.	01/10/1915	01/10/1915
War Diary	Noeux-Les-Mines.	01/10/1915	01/10/1915
War Diary	Labuissiere.	02/10/1915	02/10/1915
War Diary	Noeux-Les-Mines.	02/10/1915	02/10/1915
War Diary	Labuissiere.	03/10/1915	03/10/1915
War Diary	Lillers.	03/10/1915	03/10/1915
War Diary	Lapugnoy.	04/10/1915	04/10/1915
War Diary	Allouagne.	04/10/1915	04/10/1915
War Diary	Vaudricourt	04/10/1915	04/10/1915
War Diary	Lillers.	04/10/1915	04/10/1915
War Diary	Lapugnoy.	05/10/1915	05/10/1915
War Diary	Allouagne.	05/10/1915	05/10/1915
War Diary	Vaudricourt.	05/10/1915	05/10/1915
War Diary	Lillers.	05/10/1915	05/10/1915
War Diary	Lapugnoy.	06/10/1915	06/10/1915
War Diary	Allouagne.	06/10/1915	06/10/1915
War Diary	Maries-Les-Mines.	06/10/1915	06/10/1915
War Diary	Lapugnoy	07/10/1915	07/10/1915
War Diary	Allouagne.	07/10/1915	07/10/1915
War Diary	Marles-Les-Mines.	07/10/1915	07/10/1915
War Diary	Lapugnoy.	08/10/1915	08/10/1915
War Diary	Allouagne.	08/10/1915	08/10/1915
War Diary	Marles-Les-Mines	08/10/1915	08/10/1915
War Diary	Lillers.	08/10/1915	08/10/1915

War Diary	Lapugnoy.	09/10/1915	09/10/1915
War Diary	Allouagne.	09/10/1915	09/10/1915
War Diary	Marles-Les-Mines.	09/10/1915	09/10/1915
War Diary	Lillers.	09/10/1915	09/10/1915
War Diary	Lapugnoy.	10/10/1915	10/10/1915
War Diary	Allouagne.	10/10/1915	10/10/1915
War Diary	Marles-Les-Mines.	10/10/1915	10/10/1915
War Diary	Lapugnoy.	11/10/1915	11/10/1915
War Diary	Allouagne.	11/10/1915	11/10/1915
War Diary	Marles-Les-Mines.	11/10/1915	11/10/1915
War Diary	Lapugnoy.	12/10/1915	12/10/1915
War Diary	Allouagne. to Hallicourt.	12/10/1915	12/10/1915
War Diary	Marles-Les-Mines.	12/10/1915	12/10/1915
War Diary	Lillers. to Lozinghem.	12/10/1915	12/10/1915
War Diary	Lapugnoy.	13/10/1915	13/10/1915
War Diary	Hallicourt.	13/10/1915	13/10/1915
War Diary	Marles-Les-Mines.	13/10/1915	13/10/1915
War Diary	Lozinghem.	13/10/1915	13/10/1915
War Diary	Lapugnoy.	14/10/1915	14/10/1915
War Diary	Hallicourt.	14/10/1915	14/10/1915
War Diary	Marles-Les-Mines.	14/10/1915	14/10/1915
Miscellaneous	Lozinghem to Labeuvriere	14/10/1915	14/10/1915
War Diary	Lapugnoy.	15/10/1915	15/10/1915
War Diary	Hallicourt.	15/10/1915	15/10/1915
War Diary	Marles-Les-Mines to Houchin.	15/10/1915	15/10/1915
War Diary	Labeuvriere.	15/10/1915	15/10/1915
War Diary	Lapugnoy to Noeux-Les-Mines.	16/10/1915	16/10/1915
War Diary	Noeux-Les-Mines.	16/10/1915	16/10/1915
War Diary	Houchin.	16/10/1915	16/10/1915
War Diary	Hallicourt.	16/10/1915	16/10/1915
War Diary	Noeux-Les-Mines.	17/10/1915	17/10/1915
War Diary	Hallicourt.	17/10/1915	17/10/1915
War Diary	Noeux-Les-Mines.	18/10/1915	18/10/1915
War Diary	Houchain.	18/10/1915	18/10/1915
War Diary	Hallicourt.	18/10/1915	18/10/1915
War Diary	Noeux-Les-Mines.	19/10/1915	19/10/1915
War Diary	Houchain.	19/10/1915	19/10/1915
War Diary	Hallicourt.	19/10/1915	19/10/1915
War Diary	Noeux-Les-Mines.	20/10/1915	20/10/1915
War Diary	Houchain.	20/10/1915	20/10/1915
War Diary	Haillicourt.	20/10/1915	20/10/1915
War Diary	Noeux-Les-Mines.	21/10/1915	21/10/1915
War Diary	Houchain.	21/10/1915	21/10/1915
War Diary	Noeux-Les-Mines.	21/10/1915	22/10/1915
War Diary	Houchin.	22/10/1915	22/10/1915
War Diary	Noeux-Les-Mines.	22/10/1915	23/10/1915
War Diary	Vermelles.	23/10/1915	23/10/1915
War Diary	Noeux-Les-Mines.	23/10/1915	24/10/1915
War Diary	Vermelles.	24/10/1915	24/10/1915
War Diary	Houchin.	24/10/1915	24/10/1915
War Diary	Noeux-Les-Mines.	24/10/1915	25/10/1915
War Diary	Houchin.	25/10/1915	25/10/1915
War Diary	Noeux-Les-Mines.	25/10/1915	26/10/1915
War Diary	Vermelles.	26/10/1915	26/10/1915
War Diary	Houchin.	26/10/1915	26/10/1915
War Diary	Noeux-Les-Mines.	26/10/1915	27/10/1915

War Diary	Houchin.	27/10/1915	27/10/1915
War Diary	Noeux-Les-Mines.	27/10/1915	28/10/1915
War Diary	Houchin.	28/10/1915	28/10/1915
War Diary	Noeux-Les-Mines.	28/10/1915	29/10/1915
War Diary	Vermelles.	29/10/1915	29/10/1915
War Diary	Houchin.	29/10/1915	29/10/1915
War Diary	Noeux-Les-Mines.	29/10/1915	30/10/1915
War Diary	Houchin.	30/10/1915	30/10/1915
War Diary	Noeux-Les-Mines.	30/10/1915	31/10/1915
War Diary	Houchin.	31/10/1915	31/10/1915
War Diary	Noeux-Les-Mines.	31/10/1915	31/10/1915
Heading	15th Division F.A.W.U. Vol 5 Nov 15		
War Diary	Noeux-Les-Mines.	01/11/1915	25/11/1915
War Diary	Gosnay.	26/11/1915	30/11/1915
Heading	15th Division 15th F.A.W.U. Vol 6 Decr 15		
War Diary	Gosnay.	01/12/1915	14/12/1915
War Diary	Lillers	15/12/1915	31/12/1915
Miscellaneous			
Heading	15th F.A.W.U. Vol 7 January 1916		
War Diary	Lillers.	01/01/1916	14/01/1916
War Diary	Lillers to Noeux-Les-Mines.	15/01/1916	15/01/1916
War Diary	Noeux-Les-Mines.	16/01/1916	31/01/1916
Heading	15th Div F.A.W.U. Feb 1916		
Heading	15th F.A.W.U. Vol 8		
War Diary	Noeux-Les-Mines.	01/02/1916	29/02/1916
Heading	War Diary Of 15th Divisional Field Ambulance-Workshop Unit A.S.C. For the month of March 1916		
Heading	15 Div F.A.W.U Vol 9		
War Diary	Noeux-Les-Mines.	01/03/1916	26/03/1916
War Diary	Lillers.	27/03/1916	31/03/1916

WO95/1932/3

15TH DIVISION

15TH FLD AMB WORKSHOP UNIT.

JLY 1915 - MAR 1916

131/6250

15th Division.

15th Ambulance Workshop Unit

Vol. I

9-31-7-15

W/T. R.M.
M24 R.M.
July 1915

MEMORANDUM.

WAR DIARY

15th Div'al Field Ambulance
Workshop Unit.

From July 9th 1915 – July 31st 1915.

B E Sutton Lt A.S.C.
15th Div'al F.A.W.S.

July 9th 1915. Friday

The following Embarked on SS "Santa Isobel"
leaving 4.20 a.m.

        Lt B.E. Sutton O.C.
    M. Staff-Sergeant Cutler
Sergts. Bowler, Barker & Lloyd.
   Cpls. Chamberlin & Banham
Lce. Cpls. Prince, Blaxton, Johnson & Bell.
Privates. Barfield, Aldus, Booth, Bradley,
       Dixon, Burgoyne, Cook, Cousins,
       Cribb, Cottrell, Cannon, Ellis,
       Goddard, Jones, Perry, Spenser,
       Shaw, Pitt & Wood.

All vehicles, consisting of 21 ambulances,
1 workshop lorry, 1 Store lorry, 1 30 cwt lorry,
1 car & 3 motor cycles were on board, also
4 6" B.L. Guns.

The following left Southampton (with the 15th Divl Amml
Park) on the S.S. "Golden Eagle"
Sergts. Franklin, Skey & Wright.
Lce Cpls. Penman & Hicks
Privates. Allthorpe, Cornick, Cannon, Clayton, Drury,
Davies, Gillen, Grant C., Groom, Goss, Hirst, Hardy,
Harries, James, Johnson A., Keightley, Kinnaird, Lake,
Lambert, Ogden, Parker, Pitt, Rayment, Ratcliffe, Rouse,
Sugg, Tuckwell, Grant J.R. & Bodden.
Pte Rutter left behind at Avonmouth hospital
Pte Rose left behind at Bristol hospital.

       B E Sutton Lt R.A.M.C. 15th Divl
                               Train.

July 10th Saturday.

The S.S. "Golden Eagle" arrived at Rouen in the morning. The 34 N.C.O's & men disembarked there & went into the Rest camp to await arrival of rest of Unit & vehicles.

The S.S. Santa Isobel arrived at Havre in evening but as the 4, 6" guns had to be unloaded there it was impossible to go on to Rouen till they had been unloaded. All slept on board the S.S. Santa Isobel.

B E Sutton Lt. A.S.C.
15th Div'l Fd. Amb
Workshop Unit

July 11th 1915. Sunday.

A few of the vehicles unloaded at Havre to allow of access to the guns.
Reported arrival & received instructions to proceed by road to Rouen - from the A.D. of T. at Havre.
Wolseley Ambulance (chassis No 23522) (W.D. No 15072) had radiator badly damaged by one of the 6" guns during unloading. Several of the other vehicles suffered slight damage, but nothing so serious as the above.
Obtained petrol in evening.
Unloading not nearly completed, so placed guard on few unloaded vehicles & again slept on board.

B E Sutton Lt A.S.C.
15th Divnl F.A & W.Co

July 12th Monday.

Unloading of vehicles proceeded and was finished in evening.
Obtained pass & route from D.A.D. of T. at Havre & got ready to start for Rouen at 7 a.m. next day.
Sgt Barker & Pte Barfield repaired rear spring on Sunbeam car. This had been broken at Avonmouth Docks just prior to embarkation.
Men all slept in vehicles on the quay.

B. E. Sutton Lt. A.S.C.
1st Div'l T. & S. C.

July 13th Tuesday

Started punctually at 7 a.m. for Rouen.
Only 1 man was available as driver
for each car, but an excellent run
was made though one or two of the
men had hardly driven before
Arrived at Rouen 12.45 p.m.
Reported arrival to D.D of T. (Colonel
Hazelton) & received instructions as to
completion of kit & equipment &c.
After the men had had lunch,
Lieut Forbes conducted us to the Rest
Camp where we joined the rest of the
Unit.
Vehicles were all cleaned & kit
inspection held.

D E Sutton Lt A.S.C.
15th Div'l S:T & W.S.

July 14 Wednesday.

Medical inspection of 29 N.C.O's & men in morning. Other 24 men had been examined previously. All passed.
Pte. Wood inoculated for 2nd time.
Drew clothing & equipment from Ordnance Stores in morning. Issued same in afternoon.
Drew petrol & filled up all tanks, & left 4 gals on each ambulance & 10 gals on each lorry as reserve.
Very heavy rain impeded drawing of stores, & necessitated moving all the cars.
Prepared men & vehicles for inspection

B E Sutton Lt A.S.C.

July 15th Thursday.   7

Men & vehicles inspected by Lt Forbes, vice Col Hazelton. Received orders to move to a square in another part of the city on the road to Abbeville for the night.
Moved off at 2 p.m. & parked vehicles. Drew M.T. Stores from M.T. Depot in afternoon with Karrier Lorry. Could get very little that was required, & was unable to replace damaged Wolseley Radiator or Sunbeam rear Spring.
Reported to A.D. of T. & Base Commandant & received definite instructions, pass & route to Abbeville. Vehicles renumbered.

B E Sutton Lt M.T.A.S.C.

July 16. Friday.

Moved off to Abbeville at 8.30 a.m.
One Ford ambulance punctured rear tyre in morning.

The 30 cwt Harrier lorry broke down within 7 kilometres of Abbeville, owing to a cylinder water jacket cracking, allowing the water to get down into the crank case, thus mixing with the lubricating oil, & resulting in a big-end bearing running out.

The workshop lorry towed the Harrier into Abbeville.

Incessant rain all day.

Parked vehicles & settled down the men in the Rest Camp at Abbeville.

Reported arrival to D.D. of T. & Base Commandant.

Exchanged Harrier lorry No 11481 for another lorry of the same make (an old Type B.80. No 8866) at 317 Co. M.T. A.S.C.

Obtained new radiator for Wolseley Ambulance at Advanced M.T. Depôt.

Received instructions, route to St Omer & pass from Base Commandant.

B.E. Sutton Lt. A.S.C.

July 17th ~~Friday~~. Saturday.

Left Abbeville for St Omer at 8 a.m.
Had trouble with lubrication of newly received
Karrier, which necessitated taking down sump
& cleaning oil filters on the road.
This effected marked improvement, though
this lorry was in bad condition & required
thorough overhaul.
About 3 kilometres from St Omer Pte. Dixon
on No 21 Ford collided with a horse belonging
to the R.F.A. seriously damaging radiator, lamp,
& wing. Towed this car into St Omer.
Reported arrival to D.A.D.M.S. at St Omer, &
parked vehicles in cattle market.

B E Sutton Lt.A.S.C.

July. 18th Sunday.

Replaced radiators on Ford & Wolseley ambulances, also fitted new brake linings on Ford Ambulance No 21. Straightened wing on same ambulance.

D.A.D.M.S. inspected ambulances & gave instructions to have windows made in front of Wolseleys for ventilation & also ordered the removal of the two top stretchers & structures for supporting same on the Fords.

This work was immediately put in hand.

Reported to D.D. of S.T. & received instructions with reference to taking a census of the Vehicles with Unit at 6 p.m. on this date.

Completed & handed in Census.

On the instructions of the D.A.D.M.S. I took No 1 Section (Sgt. Skey) to Houchin.

Two ambulances were left with the 45th Field Ambulance at Husdigneul (one to proceed to Allouagne on the next day) & five to Drouvain near HOUCHIN.

B E Sutton T.H.S.C.

July. 19th Monday.

Vehicles inspected by Capt. Rendell. occupying the whole day.

Sgt. SKEYS having left the previous day could not be inspected.

Sgts. WRIGHT & LLOYD were both complimented on the cleanliness & mechanical fitness of all their vehicles.

Several defects were revealed on the Harrier lorry, which was just taken over by us at ABBEVILLE a few days before. No opportunity had occurred to look over this lorry.

The Sunbeam car also required new clutch spigot bush, a rear spring, & the rear brake rod had too much side play.

With these two exceptions all the vehicles were in perfect condition, though a few items requiring adjustment were noted. Wolseley magneto couplings were the principal offenders.

Received instructions from D.A.D.M.S. to proceed to Gosnay in the evening, but could not get finished in time. Prepared for early start in morning.

Relined footbrake on no 15 Wolseley. Fitters Ptes. Parker & Lake.

B.G. Sutton Lt.A.S.C.

July. 20th Tuesday.

Left ST. OMER at 9 a.m. with Sects.
No 2 & 3 & workshop Unit. Ford No 21. (Pte Bull)
punctured near ALLOUAGNE.
Arrived at GOSNAY about 1.45. Reported to
A.D.M.S. at 15th Divl Headquarters & then
parked cars & workshop etc on grass
plot adjoining chateau at Hesdigneul.
Ambulances all cleaned. Cpl Chamberlin
& Pte. Barfield worked on windows for
Wolseley bodies.

B E Sutton Lt A.S.C.

July 21. Wednesday.

All Wolseley drivers were detailed to paint the hoods of their ambulances & to reduce the white background of the Red Cross.

This work was unfinished at the end of the day when we had hoped to get the ambulances to their allotted sections.

I went to Railhead (LILLERS) in morning to procure rations.

Filled up vehicles with petrol, oil etc ready for moving off to Field Ambulances next day.

Men bivouaced under tarpaulins etc.

B E Sutton ℒt A.S.C.

July. 22nd Thursday.

14

Took no 2 section with Sgt FRANKLIN to join the 46th Field Ambulance at ALLOUAGNE in morning.

Took no 3 section with Sgt BOWLER to HOUCHIN in evening.

No 17 ambulance. 147th Fd. Ambulance proceeded from HOUCHIN to NOEUX-LES-MINES on evacuating duty from 8.30 p.m - 9.30 p.m.

WORSHOP.

Fitted new clips to pressure pipe on no 16 Wolseley. Fitter Pte Parker.

Tightened magneto coupling on no 17 Wolseley done by driver.

Magneto coupling tightened & starting handle straightened on no 18 Wolseley. Fitter Pte Grant.

Spring clips tightened & foot brake shoes adjusted on no 19 Wolseley. Fitter Pte Lake.

Front spring clips tightened on Ford no 20. Fitter Pte Ratcliffe.

Front springs clips tightened, torque rod bolts tightened, new plug fitted. Fitter Pte Parker.

No 1 Sect. 46th Fld Amb. Cars nos 2 & 3 proceeded at 10.30 p.m. to NOEUX-LES-MINES then to SAILLIE-LA-BOURSE & back to HESDIGNEUL at 3 AM.

B.C. Sutton Lt A.S.C.

July 23rd Friday.   15

WORKSHOP. Work on Karrier 30 cwt lorry. Square on steering box tightened, fan pulley tightened, near & off side rear spring clips tightened, steering box tightened in frame, front axle bolts tightened, new bolt in gear box casing, chassis removed & reversed, back wheels tightened. Petrol carrier fixed. Fitters. Ptes Grant & Lake. Wheeler Cpl Chamberlin.
Made phosphor-bronze washers for lightning conductors for R.E. 15th Signal Service. Turner Pte Ratcliffe.
Centre spring bolt on no 2 Sunbeam replaced & spring reassembled. Fitters Lake & Parker.
Rear Lamp on no 2 Sunbeam repaired. Pte Knightley.
Generator on no 7 Ford & Motor cycle lamp repaired. Pte Knightley.

NO 1. SECTION   No detail

No 2. SECTION. No 12 Ambulance proceeded at 11.30 A.M. to CHOCQUES, returned to ALLOUAGNE 1 p.m. on Duty Case.
No 13 car proceeded at 10 A.M. to LILLERS. returned to ALLOUAGNE 11 a.m. Staff Duty.
No 14 car to Hd Qrs & return to ALLOUAGNE from 9.30 a.m. to 10.30 a.m. Staff duty

No 3 SECTION. No Detail

B E Sutton Lt A.S.C.

24th July. Saturday.

WORKSHOP. Adjusted steering on workshop Lorry. Repaired Speedometer wheel. Tightened up Brake Drum, side brakes, supporting nuts for gear box. Fitters Ptes. Lake & Parker. Handles crossed on 14 Petrol Cans, & cans painted black & marked "W" & "O" for Water & Oil. Pte Knightley.

NO 1 SECTION. No 5 ambulance proceeded to ST OMER at 2 p.m. Returned 7.30 p.m.

NO 2 SECTION. No Detail.

NO 3. SECTION. No Detail.

B E Sutton Lt A.S.C

July 25th. Sunday.

WORKSHOP. Store lorry. Petrol pipe tightened on tank, band of footbrake lined up with drum, side brake levercot to clear chain, spring clips tightened.
Half workshop staff under M. Staff Sergeant Cutler went to the Baths at BROUAY.

No 1 SECTION. No 7 Ambulance out from 9.45 a.m to 11.30 a.m. proceeded to LABEUVRIÈRE
No 7. proceeded to LILLERS from 3 p.m. to 5 p.m.
No 7. proceeded to LABEUVRIÈRE from 6 p.m to 6.40 p.m.

No 2 SECTION No Detail

No 3 SECTION Ambulances Nos. 19, 20, 21 Proceeded from HOUCHIN to NOEUX LES MINES for General instructions for Medical Orderlies, & finding positions of Regimental Aid Posts. 6 Drivers were taken for this purpose. Returned 26/7/15.

B Sutton Lt A.S.C.

July 26th Monday.

WORKSHOP. Replaced centre spring bolt on No 10 Sunbeam. Fitters Ptes Grant & Lake.
Repaired petrol pipe on Vauxhall for Hd Qrs. Fitter Pte Lake.
Half workshop staff went to baths at BROUAY under Sgt Barker.

No1 SECTION. No 4 car proceeded to LABEUVRIERE at 3 p.m. Returned at 3.50 p.m.

No 2. SECTION. No 10 Ambulance proceeded to LAPUGNOY at 11. AM. Returned 12. M.D. Broke rear spring bolt

No 3 SECTION. No Detail.

Rubbed off old numbers & painted correct ones on the Ambulances of No 1 section.
Wheelers. Cpl Chamberlin & Pte Barfield.

B E Sutton T.K.C.

July 27. Tuesday.

WORKSHOP. Started overhauling Karrier lorry.
Removed cylinders & dismantled gear box.
Fitters on Engine. Ptes Grant, Ratcliffe
Fitters on Gear Box Ptes Lake & Parker.

NO 1 SECTION. N° 5 Ambulance proceeded to
LILLERS at 2 p.m. returned at 4.30 p.m.
Cpl Banham, driver i/c, reported slight
accident in which offside front wing
was slightly damaged on this journey.

N° 2. SECTION
No 9 ambulance proceeded to LILLERS at 2 p.m. returned at 3 p.m.
No 10 ambulance proceeded to GOSNAY at 10:30 A.M. returned 3 p.m.
No 11 ambulance proceeded to MARLES-LES-MINES at 2 p.m. returned at 3 p.m.
No 13 ambulance proceeded to LAPUGNOY at 10 a.m. returned at 11:30 A.M.
Motor cycle Orderly work.

N° 3. SECTION. No Detail

In morning I went with M.S. Sergeant
Cutter to inspect No 2 Section at ALLOUAGNE

B E Sutton Lt A.S.C.

July 28th Wednesday.

WORKSHOP. Proceeded with overhauling Karrier. Big ends being taken up, gear box cleaned. Filters Ptes Grant, Ratcliffe, Lake & Parker. Wing repaired on No 5 Sunbeam. Wheeler Cpl. Chamberlin.

No 1 SECTION.   No detail.

No 2 SECTION. No 11 ambulance proceeded to CHOCQUES at 6.30 A.M. Returned at 8.15 a.m. No 14 ambulance proceeded to FOUQUIERES ~~& returned~~ at 5.30 p.m. Returned at 8.30 p.m. Motor Cycle. General Duties.

No 3 SECTION. No detail

In evening I inspected No 1 Section at HESDIGNEUL with M.S. Sergt Cutter.

B E Sutton Lt A.V.C.

29th July. Thursday

WORKSHOP. Continued work on Karrier. Big-ends very bad & crankshaft journals out of truth. Ground in valves, assembled cylinders, tightened up & adjusted change speed cover & gate. Fitters Ptes. Grant, Ratcliffe, Lake & Parker.
Took down clutch of No 5 Sunbeam ambulance, refaced same in lathe, reassembled it & tested car. Fitter Sgt Barker, Turner Ratcliffe. Tested by M.S. Sergt. Cutler.

NO 1 SECTION. No 3. ambulance proceeded to Divnl Hd Qrs at 3 p.m. then to LABUISSIERE, & returned at 4 p.m.
        No 4 ambulance proceeded to BETHUNE at 2 p.m. returned at 3.30 p.m.

NO 2 SECTION No 13 ambulance proceeded to BUSNES at 6 p.m. returned at 8 p.m. Motor Cycle messages & letters.

NO 3 SECTION. No Detail.

I went with M.S. Sergt Cutler to inspect No 2 section at ALLOUAGNE.

B E Sutton Lt A.S.C.

30th July. Friday.

WORKSHOP.

Finished off Karrier. Assembled water pipes, carburetter, &c; erected gear-box. Repaired brake-shoes, preparing lorry for testing. Fitters Ptes. Grant, Ratcliffe, Lake & Parker, Sergt Barker. Blacksmiths Ptes Clayton & Hardy. ~~Tested~~ Engine run in for one hour. Lorry tested by M.S. Sergt Cutler from 7pm to 8pm. Pick-axes and shovels fitted on all three lorries by Cpl Chamberlin & Pte Barfield. Petrol cans altered & painted black & lettered for No 2 Section. Pte Knightley.

<u>No 1 SECTION.</u> No 5 ambulance proceeded to LILLERS at 2·15 pm. returned at 4·40 pm.

No 4 ambulance proceeded to BETHUNE at 2·30 pm. returned at 3·30 pm.

No 6 ambulance proceeded to GOSNAY at 3·15 p.m. returned at 4·15 p.m.

<u>No 2 SECTION</u> No 8 ambulance proceeded from ALLOUAGNE to CHOCQUES at 8·15 a.m. returned to VAUDRICOURT at 3 p.m.

No 2 Section moved from ALLOUAGNE to VAUDRICOURT calling at the workshops for alteration of numbers on way. Wheelers Cpl Chamberlin & Pte Barfield

<u>No 3 SECTION.</u> No detail.

B E Sutton Lt A.S.C.

July. 31. Saturday.

WORKSHOP. Tightened Chains on Karrier lorry, & adjusted tappets. Fitter Pte Grant, making Valve-grinding tools for Sunbeams & Fords for No 2 Section. Blacksmiths, Pte Parker altering Handles of petrol tins for oil & water for No section. Pte Knightley.

Altering numbers on ambulances of No 3 section, altering window in store lorry, & making box for petrol, oil & water cans on Ford ambulance. Cpl Chamberlin & Pte Barfield.

SECTION NO. 1. No 7 ambulance proceeded to LILLERS at 9 a.m. returned at 11 a.m.

No 6 ambulance proceeded to GOSNAY at 11.5 a.m. returned at 11.45 a.m.

No. 3. ambulance proceeded to LILLERS at 10.5 a.m. returned 12.45 p.m.

No 2 ambulance proceeded to LAPUGNOY returned to HESDIGNEUL then proceeded to LAPUGNOY again. Out at 10.45 a.m. returned 12.45 p.m.

SECTION No 3. Ambulances No's 15. 16. 17. 18. 19 & 20. Proceeded from HOUCHIN to workshops at HESDIGNEUL for alterations of Numbers & oil & water cans. Returned 5 p.m.

No 21 ambulance proceeded to LILLERS at 2 p.m. returned 7 p.m.

SECTION No 2. No 12 ambulance proceeded to CHOCQUES & LILLERS at 3.45 p.m. Returned 6 p.m.

No 14. ambulance proceeded on general duty to GOSNAY & District. Out from 11.30 a.m. to 9.30 p.m.

B E Sutton Lt A.S.C.
15th Div'l Fd. Amb. W'k'p

121/6753

15th Burma

15th Sikh F.A. Bankok's Unit
Vol: II

August 15

WAR DIARY
INTELLIGENCE SUMMARY

(Erase heading not required.)

Army Form C. 2118.

15th Div¹ Field Ambulance Workshop April 1917

Place	Date	Hour	Summary of Events and Information	Remarks and references to Appendices
HESDIGNEUL	10/8/15		WORKSHOP. Repairing Damaged Stretchers. Radiators for Stoves. Pte KNIGHTLEY and PARKER. Fixing Lamp Brackets & Shed. Lawson Workshop and Pte Lowis. Pte CLAYTON & HARDY	
"	"		No 1 SECTION. Amb. No 1 Left HOUCHIN at 12 noon for HESDIGNEUL & returned to HOUCHIN at 2.30 pm	
"	"		Amb. No 7. Left HOUCHIN at 9.30 p.m. for HESDIGNEUL returned to HOUCHIN 10.50 p.m.	
"	"		Ambs. Nos 4, 5 & 6 proceeded to NOEUX-LES-MINES at 8.40 a.m. returning to HESDIGNEUL 9.20 a.m.	
"	"		" " " " " " " " " " - 6.10 P.m	
"	"		Amb. No 1 proceeded to BETHUNE at 12 p.m. & returned to HESDIGNEUL at 3.35 P.m.	
"	"		Amb. No 2 proceeded to HOUCHIN at 2.40 p.m. & returned to HESDIGNEUL at 3.55 p.m.	
"	"		Amb. No 7 proceeded from HOUCHIN at 12.15 p.m. to HESDIGNEUL, returning to HOUCHIN at 2.30 p.m.	
"	"		" " 7 " " " " " " " " " " 8.30 p.m.	
"	"		" " " " " " " " " " " " 6.20 p.m.	
"	"		No 2 SECTION. Amb No 12 proceeded from DROUVIN to GOSNAY at 11.15 a.m. returning at 12.35 pm	
"	"		Amb. No 13 proceeded to LILLERS at 2.10 p.m. returning to VAUDRICOURT at 4.40 P.M.	
"	"		Amb. No 14 " " GOSNAY " 12 noon " " " 1 P.M	
"	"		Amb. No 14 " " " " 3 p.m. " " " 4 P.M	
"	"		Amb. No 14 " " BETHUNE " 4 p.m. " " " 8 p.m. with Medical Stores.	

Army Form C. 2118.

WAR DIARY
or
INTELLIGENCE SUMMARY.

(Erase heading not required.)

15th Divnl F.A.S.n. A.S.M.Z

Place	Date	Hour	Summary of Events and Information	Remarks and references to Appendices
	10/8/15 (Con.d)		No 3 SECTION.	
			Car No. Mileage Evacuating Patients Duty Remarks	
			15 4 3 Collecting	
			16 12 1 "	
			17 No detail	
			18 4 2 Collecting	
			I went with Sgt BARKER and Pte COOK to LILLERS to get M.T. stores from Railhead. A new body Radiator was sent by mistake returned next day.	
	10/8/15		Car No. Mileage Patients Remarks	
			19 3 2 Collecty	
			20 32 5 Collecty evacuating	
			21 24 55 Evacuating Advd Stations	
			R.B.Hutton Lt A.C.	

Army Form C. 2118.

WAR DIARY
or
INTELLIGENCE SUMMARY.

(Erase heading not required.) 15th British Field Ambulance Workshop Wed. 11.8.15

Wednesday Aug 11th 1915

Place	Date	Hour	Summary of Events and Information	Remarks and references to Appendices
HESDIGNEUL	11/8/15		WORKSHOP. Fitting & fixing lamp brackets & lamps on workshop & stove lorries. Pte. CLAYTON & HARDY Repairing radiator (notably) for Stove. Pte. KNIGHTLEY and PARKER. Making spanners for Sunbeam jets, for No 1 & No 2 Section. Ptes. CLAYTON & HARDY. No 1 SECTION. Amb. No 2 proceeded to CHOCQUES at 3.30 p.m. returned to HESDIGNEUL at 4.40 p.m. " No 1 " LILLERS at 2.30 p.m. " " " 4.30 p.m. " No 7 " BROUAY at 8.30 p.m. " " " 9.50 p.m. Ambs. Nos 4, 5, 6 " NOEUX-LES-MINES at 8.30 a.m. " " " 10.0 a.m. Amb. No 7. Lgt. HOUCHIN at 12 noon, proceeded to HESDIGNEUL & returned at 2.20 p.m. " " " " " 6.45 p.m. " " " 8.45 p.m. No 2 SECTION Amb. No 12 proceeded to HESDIGNEUL at 2 p.m. returned to VAUDRICOURT at 4 p.m. (Workshop for Petrol) " 13 " DROUVIN " 4.30 p.m. " " " 4.50 p.m. " 14 " AIRE " 8.a.m. " " " 2 p.m. No 3 SECTION. Car No. Mileage Patients Remarks At No Village Patients Remarks 15 No Detail 19 13 2 Collecting & Evacuating 16 No Detail 20 20 4 Evacuating 17 10 2 Evacuating 21 3 1 Collecting 18 No Detail	

Army Form C. 2118.

WAR DIARY
or
INTELLIGENCE SUMMARY.

(Erase heading not required.) 15th D:S: Field Ambulance Works by field H.Q. A.Q.

Instructions regarding War Diaries and Intelligence Summaries are contained in F. S. Regs., Part II. and the Staff Manual respectively. Title pages will be prepared in manuscript.

Aug 11th 1915 (Cont)

Place	Date	Hour	Summary of Events and Information	Remarks and references to Appendices
NESDIGNEUL	11/8/15		Drew 540 fo fm Field Cashier 9th Corps in morning. Paid men in afternoon. SGT. BARKER & Lee/Cpl PRINCE proceeded to LILLERS in afternoon with loose leg Radiator of the M.T. unserviceable Char-a-banc to be returned to Base M.T. Depôt. No M/2 0/3386 Pte Rose (Turner + Fitter) rejoined the Unit.	
	11/8/15			B. Butler Lt. H.C

Army Form C. 2118.

WAR DIARY
or
INTELLIGENCE SUMMARY.

(Erase heading not required.) 15th Field Amb. 5th Division Ambulance 2nd batch Irish

Place	Date	Hour	Summary of Events and Information	Remarks and references to Appendices
HESDIGNEUL	12/9/15	9.30 a.m.		
		3.30 pm	Douglas Hyde in 3 SECTION taking down Engine, Cleaning Cylinders, pistons, grinding in valves. Testing. Ptes GRANT and RATCLIFFE. Making Sanitary Utensils for A.D.M.S. Ptes KNIGHTLEY & PARKER.	
		2 pm	Sunbeam Gen. Car. taking down Back Springs, bolting Broken leaf, setting up Springs. Ptes KARRIN, LORRY. Adjusting Gears. Pte LAKE. CLAYTON & HARDY. NO. 1 SECTION.	
			Amb. hos. 4,596 proceeded to NOEUX-LES-MINES at 8.20 a.m. & returned to HESDIGNEUL at 9.25 a.m.	10.15 a.m.
			" " 1 " " GOSNAY " 9.35 a.m.	11.5 a.m.
			" " 1 " " GOSNAY " 10.25 a.m.	12 noon.
			" " 6 " " ALLOUAGNE " 10. a.m.	3.0 p.m.
			" " 2 " " GOSNAY " 2.30 p.m.	6.35 p.m.
			" " 5 " " MAZINGARBE " 3.15 p.m.	6.45 p.m.
			" " 4,596 " " NOEUX-LES-MINES " 5.30 p.m.	8.45 p.m.
			" " 1 " " VERMELLES " 7.5 p.m.	
			Amb. hos 7 left HOUCHIN at 12 noon proceeded to HESDIGNEUL & returned to HOUCHIN at 12.35 p.m.	
			" " 7 " " " 1.15 p.m.	2.45 p.m.
			" " 7 " " " 7.15 p.m.	9.5 p.m.

WAR DIARY
or
INTELLIGENCE SUMMARY.

Army Form C. 2118.

Aug. 12 1915 (Cont)

Place	Date	Hour	Summary of Events and Information	Remarks and references to Appendices
	12/8/15		No 2 SECTION.	
			No 1 D Amb. forwarded to HESDIGNEUL at 2 p.m. returned to VAUDRICOURT at 4.30 p.m.	
			No 12 " - " GOSNAY - 6 p.m. " - 7/6 p.m.	
			No 13 - " - " CHOCQUES - 8 a.m. " - 10.35 p.m.	
			No 13 - " - " LILLERS - 5.10 p.m. " - 7.10 p.m.	
			No 3 SECTION. Evacuating Duties.	
			Car No Trilage Patients Remarks Car No Village Patients Remarks	
			15 - 13 5 Evacuating 19 30 10 Collecting/Evacuating	
			16 10 2 Evacuating 20 24 2 Evacuating	
			17 No Detail 21 30 — Medical Stores	
			18 18 3 Collecting/Evacuating	

B Shuttn Capt A.C.

Army Form C. 2118

WAR DIARY
or
INTELLIGENCE SUMMARY.
(Erase heading not required.)

Aug 13th Friday

Place	Date	Hour	Summary of Events and Information	Remarks and references to Appendices
	13/8/15	3.30pm – 4.0pm	WORKSHOP. Sunbeam Open Car. Setting up rear & front springs & replacing same. Ptes CLAYTON & HARDY. Sunbeam – . Taking down Clutch, brake rods, rebearing kingpin. Ptes BARFIELD & RATCLIFFE. Ford No.13. (No 2 Section) Adjusting top speed removing rear wheel & removing fell washers to prevent grease leakage. SGT BARKER & Pte ALLTHORPE. Austin Engine (in workshop) Removing cylinders & cleaning pistons. Pte KNIGHTLEY. Sunbeam No 4 (Hosp section) Fixing horn, fitting valance. CPL CHAMBERLIN. No 1 SECTION. Amb. No 3 proceeded to GOSNAY at 10.5 a.m. and returned to HESDIGNEUL at 10.55 a.m. " " 2 " " "LABUSSIERE" " 2.30 p.m. " " " " 3.25 p.m. " " 3 " " "NOEUX-LES-MINES" " 8.15 a.m. " " " " 9.45 a.m. " " 4, 5T6 " " " " 5.20 p.m " " " " 7.10 p.m. " " 5 " " CHOCQUES " 9.45 p.m. " " " " 10.15 p.m. Amb No 7 left HOUCHIN at 12.0 noon proceeded to HESDIGNEUL returned to HOUCHIN 2.30 pm " " 1 " " " " 7.15 pm " " " " 9.0 pm. No 2 SECTION Amb. No 8. proceeded to GOSNAY at 2.35 pm returned to VAUDRICOURT at 5.34 p.m. (2 journeys) " No 9 " " LILLERS " 2.35 pm " " " " 5.20 pm	

WAR DIARY
INTELLIGENCE SUMMARY

Army Form C. 2118

July 13th Friday (Cont) 1st A/s FA/H.A.

No 2 SECTION (Cont)

No 10 Amb - Changing to other detail
No 11. Amb. proceeded to GOSNAY at 8.45 a.m. returned to VAUDRICOURT at 9.45 p.m.
No 11. " " - LILLERS - 10.30 a.m. " - 1.0 p.m.
No 12. " " - FOUQUIERE - 8.30 a.m. " - 9.30 a.m.
No 12. " " - GOSNAY - 11.30 a.m. " - 12.30 a.m.
No 13. " " - HESDIGNEUL - 2 p.m. " - 6 p.m.   Hospitals
No 14. " " - GOSNAY - 2.30 p.m. " - 3.15 p.m.   Refuel

No 3 SECTION Evacuating Duties

Car No.	Hilage	Patients	Remarks
15	No detail		
16	No detail		
17	14	—	Nil
18	13	4	Collecting Evacuating
19	25	6	Collecting Evacuating
20	36	8	Evacuating
21	24	—	Medical Stores

B.U.R. Lt/H.A.C.

Army Form C. 2118

WAR DIARY
INTELLIGENCE SUMMARY

August 14th 1915 (Saturday) 13th Div. F.Amb. A.C.M.T.

Place	Date	Hour	Summary of Events and Information	Remarks and references to Appendices
HESDIGNEUL		12 noon to 2 pm	WORKSHOP. Sunbeam Char. Cas. Fixing springs adjusting Brakes. Pte GRANT & Pte RATCLIFFE. Audi workshop. Engine Refacing valves grinding in taps, Refacing cylinders Pte PARKER & KNIGHTLEY. Sunbeam No 10 (No 2 Section) Adjusting magneto, carburetor sparking Plugs, disconnecting examining Jacket Pipes. Staff Sergt CUTLER and Pte ALDUS.	
			No 1 SECTION Amb No 2 proceeded to CHOCQUES at 9.15 am returned to HESDIGNEUL at 10.20 a.m.	
			" " " " " NOEUX-LES-MINES - 8.36 a.m. " " " 9.15 a.m.	
			" " " " " " " " 5.20 pm " " " 7.30 pm	
			" " " 4.556 " " " " " " " "	
			Amb No 7 left HOUCHIN at 12.5 pm proceeded to HESDIGNEUL and returned to HOUCHIN at 9.25 pm	
			Amb No 7 - HOUCHIN - 7.30 pm " " " " " 9.20 pm	
			No 2 SECTION Amb No 11 proceeded to HESDIGNEUL at 11.30 a.m. returned to VAUDRICOURT at 12.30 pm.	Between the Corporal General
			Amb No 11 " " CHOCQUES " 12.35 pm " " " 2.35 pm	Repairs + Petrol
			Amb. No 12 " " HESDIGNEUL " 11 p.m. " " " 1 am	
			Amb No 13 " " DROUVIN " 8.45 a.m " " " 9.40 pm	
			Amb. No 13 " " BETHUNE & GONAY 3.45 pm " " " 6.30 pm	
			Amb No 14 " " GOSNAY " 3.0 pm " " " 4.7 am	
			M/Cycle Messenger Work.	

Army Form C. 2118.

WAR DIARY
or
INTELLIGENCE SUMMARY.

(Erase heading not required.) 13th Div. H.Q A.D.M.S M.C

August 14th (Cont)

Place	Date	Hour	Summary of Events and Information	Remarks and references to Appendices

MAZINGARBE. No.of Amb. Sittings Patients Remarks. By/Amb. Sittings Patients Remarks.
15   13   6   Collecting & evacuating   19   20   5 Collecting & evacuating
16   No Detail   20   30   6   evacuating
17   No Detail   21   14   — Awaited Orders
18   No Detail

M3/6/41 Lee Col Hanson reported his arrival in the morning, & I forthwith attached him to the 46th Field Ambulance vice Lee Col Miles.
I proceeded to MIRE in the afternoon to report to MAJOR McLEOD D.A.D.T. took weekly Returns & pointed out deficiency in personnel according to war Establishment.

B.E.M.H. H.A.C.

Army Form C. 2118

WAR DIARY

INTELLIGENCE SUMMARY

(Erase heading not required.) 15th Div[isional] L[ight] M[otor] Ambulance Workshop Unit

August 15th 1915

Place	Date	Hour	Summary of Events and Information	Remarks and references to Appendices
HESDIGNEUL	15/8/15 Sunday		R & R WORKSHOP. Repairs to carrier of Motor Cycle. No 3. Section P[te]s LAKE & PARKER. Making screw. Cpl. CHAMBERLIN. 9 P[t]e BARFIELD.	
HESDIGNEUL			No 1. SECTION 2 Journeys to HESDIGNEUL from HOUCHIN by Amb. No 7. Two Journeys to NOEUX-LES-MINES by Ambs. 4, 5 & 6.	Detail filed
VAUDRICOURT			No 2. SECTION No.13 Amb. Journeys to NOEUX-LES-MINES, HOUCHIN & BOSNAY about 21 miles. No 14 Amb Journeys to LES BREBIS & BOSNAY about 20 miles.	Detail filed
NOEUX-LES-MINES			No 3. SECTION Colliery evacuating. Amb. No. 15, 14 miles;— No 16, 8 mls;— No 17, 12 miles,— No 18, 14 mls ;— No 19, 27 mls; — No 20, 40 mls. B Shelton N.A.C.	Detail filed
HESDIGNEUL	16/8/15 Monday		WORKSHOP. Repairing Primus Stove for 4 Sta[tion] Hospital. PTE KNIGHTLEY. No 16 lorry (No 3. Section) Repairs to water pipes & adjusting tappets (10.15AM – 11.15AM.) Sergt P[T]E. Motor cycle (No 3 Section) Making & fitting footboards. Cpl CHAMBERLIN P[t]e BARFIELD. Repairs to carrier Pte PARKER. Making clips for carrying pickerwheels for toolbelt being Section. P[t]e CLAYTON HARDY Motor cycle (No 1 Section) Varnishing front forks PTE ALDUS. Varnishing rest ring for spring forks PTE RATCLIFFE	
HESDIGNEUL			No 1 SECTION Ambs Nos 4,6 & 8. 2 Journeys to NOEUX-LES-MINES. No 2. 1 Journey to LILLERS. No 7. Two journeys from HOUCHIN to HESDIGNEUL	Detail filed
VAUDRICOURT			No 2. SECTION No. 14 & Journeys to BETHUNE, DROUIN, BOSNAY, LILLERS. about 138 miles.	Detail filed

Army Form C. 2118

WAR DIARY
or
INTELLIGENCE SUMMARY.

(Erase heading not required.) 13th Div^l F.A. Col.

Aug 16th 1915.

Place	Date	Hour	Summary of Events and Information	Remarks and references to Appendices
NOEUX-LES-MINES	16/8/15	Monday	**No 3. SECTION** Collecting rose cutting. Amb No 15, 16 miles;- No 16, 32 miles;- No 19, 18 miles;- Detail field. No 20, 35 miles;- No 21, 41 miles:	
			I went with A.D.M.S. Lt DAWKES R.A.M.C. & Sergt CUTLER. Inspected all vehicles of his section at NOEUX-LES-MINES, MAZINGARBE & LES BREBIS. Noted particularly the chainless Rev-Sergt LLOYD's section at LES-BREBIS. B.Shelton M.R.A.C	
HESDIGNEUL	17/8/15	Tuesday	**MOTNSHOP.** Motor cycle (his section) having front forks & wheel, & fitting spring fork him (PT.ALDISS). Turning up Ireos for back axle. PTE. ROSE. Lanchem No 2. (No1 Sect) Taking down rear spring, fitting new centre pin, & removing PT BRANT & LAKE (3y^n - 94h.) Turning up Austin workshop Engine PTE KNIGHTLEY Ford No 20. (No 3 Sect) Taking down side brake lever repairing to Col. PT. RATCLIFFE (3.0'm to 5.0'pm) I went with M.S. & Sergt CUTLER to try RANOULT W.S. CHAINS on Lorely at MAZINGARBE in returning.	
HESDIGNEUL			**No 1. SECTION** Amb No 1. One journey to HOUCHIN. Amb No 12, 370- two journeys to NOEUX-LES-MINES. Amb Detail field. No 7.- Two journeys from HOUCHIN to HESDIGNEUL.	
MAROCOURT			**No 2. SECTION** Amb Nos 8 & 9 One journey east to GOSNAY each 6 miles;- Amb No 13 Journeys Detail field. to BETHUNE & FOUQUEREUIL, 19 miles;- Amb. No 14 Journey to DROUVIN & GOSNAY 6 miles. PTE SUGG sent home to England on special 7 days leave owing to death of his father	

Army Form C. 2118.

WAR DIARY
or
INTELLIGENCE SUMMARY.

(Erase heading not required.) 15th Div. H.Q.

Instructions regarding War Diaries and Intelligence Summaries are contained in F. S. Regs. Part II. and the Staff Manual respectively. Title pages will be prepared in manuscript.

Place	Date	Hour	Summary of Events and Information	Remarks and references to Appendices
NOEUX-LES-MINES	17/8/15		No 3 SECTION. Collecting Draweinly. Amb. No. 15, 13 mls; No 17, 10 mls; No 18, 14 mls; No 19, 23 mls; No 20, 48 mls; No 21, 20 mls.	B&lutr H.A.S.C
HESDIGNEUL	18/8/15 Wed		WORKSHOP. Fard No 21 (No 3 Sect) testing and fixing on clamp brackets, fitting two new lead lamps to Sidecar (No 1 Section) Adjusting Tappets, altering Handbrake, magneto in needle valve M.S. S/sgt CUTLER and Pte BRANT (9.30 am - 4.50 p.m.) Pte PARKER & Pte CLAYTON. 11.0 A.M. - 4.50 p.m. Weyple (No 3 sect) fixing fittings to W guard Pte LAKE & Weyck. No 1 sect Pte Taylor find wheel, straightening footrails fitting foot-boards. Cpl CHAMBERLIN & Pte ALDUS.	
HESDIGNEUL			No 1 SECTION. Amb No 2. Jnd journeys to NOEUX-LES-MINES; Amb No 4. Guy journey to LILLERS; Amb Nos 6 & 7. Two journeys from HOUCHIN to HESDIGNEUL & back.	D.E.H. Field
VAUDRICOURT			No 2 SECTION. Amb No 10. Journey to DROUVIN & GONNAY, 8 miles; Amb No 13. Guy journey to BOSNAY & Jnd D. I. Field one journey to BURNES 39 mls; Amb No 14. One journey to BURNES & one to NOEUX-LES-MINES, 34 miles.	
NOEUX-LES-MINES			No 3 SECTION. Collecting rounds. Amb. No 15, 14 mls; No 16, 34 mls; No 17, 6; No 19, 30 mls; No 20, 16 mls, No 21, 2 mls Cpl JOHNSON sick, admitted to hospital & evacuated to 45th Field Ambulance	B&lutr H.A.S.C

Army Form C. 2118

WAR DIARY
or
INTELLIGENCE SUMMARY.

(Erase heading not required.) 15th 3rd [signature]

Instructions regarding War Diaries and Intelligence Summaries are contained in F.S. Regs., Part II. and the Staff Manual respectively. Title pages will be prepared in manuscript.

Place	Date	Hour	Summary of Events and Information	Remarks and references to Appendices
HESDIGNEUL	19/8/15 Thurs		WORKSHOP. Ford No 61 No 1 Sect. Fitting new fan-belt (2.0 p.m. - 2.15 p.m.) Sergt BARKER. Wolseley No 19 (No 3 section) Removing cylinders, cleaning cylinders & pistons, grinding in valves, reassembling. Repairing rear axle chains & other jobs. Ptes GRANT, LAKE & PARKER. BARFIELD (11.30 a.m. - 6.0 p.m.) Making 2 air pipes for carburetor of Austin workshop Engine. PTE. KNIGHTLEY. Making coupling drawers for Workshop Gen. Box. Pte PARKER. Soldering Primus Stove for 45th Hospital. PTE KNIGHTLEY.	Details filed
HESDIGNEUL			No 1 SECTION. Amb No's 2, 3, 9, 6. Two journeys to NOEUX-LES-MINES; Amb No 4 one journey to VAUDRICOURT;- Amb No 7. Two journeys from HOUCHIN to HESDIGNEUL & back.	"
VAUDRICOURT			No 2 SECTION. Amb No 13. Two journeys to BOUVAY & one local, 14 miles.	"
NOEUX-LES-MINES			No 3 SECTION. Electric Ensee Lig Amb No 15, 8 mls;- No 17, 18 mls;- No 18, 22 mls;- No 19, 26 mls;- No 20, 262 mls;- No 21, 18 mls.	"
HESDIGNEUL			I went with Col CHAMBERLIN to try wood from L. CHARLES, RUE D'ARRAS, AIRE. Lieu-Col PRINCE followed in Harries lorry to test load. Half on body and half Rubt at BROUAY on Sen. Seb. Dainty lorry	RATahTACL
HESDIGNEUL	20/8/15 Frid		WORKSHOP Lurning & fitting new ping for steering long Harries lorry. Pte RATCLIFFE & GRANT. Lusbram No 9 (No 2 sect). Renewing rockers & fitting two back tires. 2.0 p.m. - 4 p.m. Sergt. CLAXTON	

2353 Wt.W2544/1454 700,000 5/15 D.D.&L. A.D.S.S. Forms/C 2118.

Army Form C. 2118

WAR DIARY
or
INTELLIGENCE SUMMARY.
(Erase heading not required.)

15th Div: al. S.P.W.C

Instructions regarding War Diaries and Intelligence Summaries are contained in F. S. Regs., Part II. and the Staff Manual respectively. Title pages will be prepared in manuscript.

Place	Date	Hour	Summary of Events and Information	Remarks and references to Appendices
HESDIGNEUL	20/8/15	Fri.	WORKSHOP (cont.) Austin Workshop Engine. Examining & tuning out vank-case. Ptes KNIGHTLEY & LAKE. Meyer (No 1 sect) Making & fitting footboards Col CHAMBERLIN & Pte BARFIELD. Sawing planks for Hand-guides Col CHAMBERLIN PTE BARFIELD. No 1 SECTION. Amb No 2, 317. Two journeys to NOEUX-LES-MINES. Amb No. 6 Journey to CHOCQUES. Amb No 1 Journey to BRUAY. Amb No 3. One journey to HOUCHIN. No 5 Amb. One Journey to GOSNAY, one to LABUISSIERE. Ambs No 2. No 4 & 5, Journey to ALLOUAGNE & then J, 4 & 5 to ALLOUAGNE. Amb No 7. Two Journeys from HOUCHIN to HESDIGNEUL & back.	Details filed
No 2 SECTION. Amb No 9. & HESDIGNEUL for Repairs, & also Amb No 14. Journey to BETHUNE, FOUQUIERES 10 miles.	Details filed
No 3 SECTION. Collecting & Evacuating. Amb No 15. 25 mls;- No 18, 28 mls;- No 17, 23 mls;- No 20, 51 mls;- No 21, 96 miles.	Details filed
Pte COUSINS. car driver, reported arrival from BASE M.T. Depot, ROUEN in morning. Issued with R.D.M.S to BETHUNE & VAUDRICOURT in evening. Inspected tyres & spots in No 2 Section. In afternoon Bought tea esp. with M.S. Capt BUTLER from M. VASSEUR-DUHAMEL at AIRE. Lee Cpl Prince took KARRIER lorry to NOEUX-LES-MINES & obtained 230 kilos of coal from the mines. B.S.M. M.X.M.A.C.	Details filed
HESDIGNEUL	21/8/15	Sat.	WORKSHOP Sunbeam No 8. (No 2 section) Examining all tyres & filling up ends. L.CE. CPL CLAXTON. Ford No 13. (No 2 sect) Putting featho inside cover. Lee Col CLAXTON. Sunbeam No 9. (No 2 section) Jacking up petrol tank	

2353. Wt W2544/1454 700,000 5/15 D. D. & L. A.D.S.S. Forms/C. 2118.

Army Form C. 2118.

WAR DIARY
or
INTELLIGENCE SUMMARY.
(Erase heading not required.)

15th Div'l T.A.T.&S.C.

Place	Date	Hour	Summary of Events and Information	Remarks and references to Appendices
HESDIGNEUL	21/8/15	Sat.	WORKSHOP (cont'd) repairing same (3.30pm – 4.30pm) Pte PARKER & KNIGHTLEY sent to AIRE in morning, taking returns & reporting to Major McLEOD, D.D.H.T. Lewis lathe, portable & associated with workshop staff to get two Star Repeat Lorries belonging to the R.F.C. out of ditch near the Refilling Point. Half workshop lieut went to Bethwad BROVA & KARRIER lorry.	Detail filed
"			No 1 SECTION. Ambs Nos 2, 3 & 6 two journeys to NOEUX-LES-MINES. Amb No 1 two journeys to GOSNAY, 9 one journey to LILLERS. Amb No 57 & 6 one journey to CHOCQUES ou to VAUDRICOURT. Amb No 1. One journey to VAUDRICOURT. from HOUCHIN to HESDIGNEUL. Amb No 5 one journey to GOSNAY.	
VAUDRICOURT			No 2 SECTION. Amb No 8, 9 & 10. One journey to HESDIGNEUL for the repairs, 6 miles. Amb Nos 10 & 11 one journey to 18 miles. Amb No 12. One journey to CHOCQUES 2 miles;- Amb Nos 12, 13 one journey to BETHUNE 6 miles, journey to LILLERS. Amb No 13. One journey, 9 6 Nos 14 two journeys to GOSNAY, 4 miles.	Details filed
NOEUX-LES-MINES			No 3 SECTION. Collecting & evacuating. Amb. No 15. 8 ambs;- No 66. 18 ambs;- No 17, 11 ambs, No 18, 14 ambs No 19, 12 ambs;- No 20, 42 ambs;- No 21, 12 ambs. Cpl Johnson rejoined MAZINGARBE Section from a St. Hospital. B. Walter M.T.A.C.	Details filed
HESDIGNEUL	22/8/15	Sun.	WORKSHOP Sunbeam No 71 (No 2 Sect) Repairing & loose heads extubed Pte PARKER. Examining gearbox Cpl CLAXTON Starting lubricating box to both converted vans. Cpl CHAMBERLIN & Pte CLAYTON. KARRIER Lorry went to Railhead (LILLERS) to fetch spring	

Army Form C. 2118.

WAR DIARY
or
INTELLIGENCE SUMMARY.
(Erase heading not required.)

[Signed] 6 Lt Col. Taylor

Instructions regarding War Diaries and Intelligence Summaries are contained in F. S. Regs., Part II. and the Staff Manual respectively. Title pages will be prepared in manuscript.

Place	Date	Hour	Summary of Events and Information	Remarks and references to Appendices
HESDIGNEUL	22/8/15 Sun.		No 1 SECTION Amb. No. 1 Two journeys to BETHUNE, One to GOSNAY, & one to DROUVIN. Amb. No 2. One journey to CHOCQUES. Amb. Nos. 2, 3 & 6 Two journeys to NOEUX-LES-MINES. Amb. No 7. Two journeys from HOUCHIN to HESDIGNEUL.	Detail filled
VAUDRICOURT			No 2 SECTION. Amb. No 8. Bus journey to MAZINGARBE, PHILOSOPHE; Amb. No. 11 Bus journey to HESDIGNEUL (workshops for rebuild); Amb. No 12. Bus journey to GOSNAY; Amb. No. 13. One journey to FOUQUEREUIL & on to MAZINGARBE. Amb. No 14. Two journeys to GOSNAY.	"
NOEUX-LES-MINES			No 3 SECTION Amb. No 15, 15a do; No 16, 15n do; No 19, 11 hrs; No 20, 10 do; No 21, 14 do B. Ect. till 6th fell	"
HESDIGNEUL	23/8/15 Mon.		WORKSHOP Repairing trumpet for violence of Sanitary Section Pt PARKER. Altogether fitting new radiator joint for KARRIER lorry. Pt RATCLIFFE. No 12 Sunbeam Solder under life Pt BRANT. Examining tyres. Cpl CLAXTON. Workshop Lorry Filling tyres french tubes Pt ALDUS. No 17 Wolseley. Removing cylinder, cleaning off carbon etc. Friday in cabs. Pts LAKE & PARKER. Sunbeam Car taken near Ypres working & replacing same. Pts CLAYTON, HARDY, GRANT, RATCLIFFE.	
HESDIGNEUL			No 1 SECTION Amb. nos 2, 3, & 6 two journeys to NOEUX-LES-MINES. Amb. No 1. Journeys to BROUAY. BETHUNE, & LILLERS. Amb. No 4. Journey to GOSNAY. Amb. No 5. Journey to VAUDRICOURT; Amb. No 6. Journey to CHOCQUES & NOEUX-LES-MINES.	"
VAUDRICOURT			No 2 SECTION Amb. No 8 Journey to BETHUNE. Amb. No 10. Journey to LILLERS. Amb. No 12 Journey to	"

WAR DIARY or INTELLIGENCE SUMMARY

Army Form C. 2118

Place	Date	Hour	Summary of Events and Information	Remarks and references to Appendices
	23/8/15 Mon		No 2 SECTION (Contd) to workshops at HESDIGNEUL, Amb. No 13. Journey to FOUQUEREUIL & GOSNAY. Amb No 14. Journey to DROUVIN & GOSNAY. No 3 SECTION. Collecting & Evacuating Amb. No 15. 8 nuls; No 16, 16 nuls; No 17, 14 nuls (to workshops for painting); No 18, 22 nuls; No 19, 3 nuls; No 20, 30 nuls; No 21, 52 nuls. B Edn Jn. VF R.A.C.	Detail filed
HESDIGNEUL	24/8/15 Tues.		WORKSHOP. No 17 to lorry. Enlisting from 23rd grinding in valves & reassembly. Pts LAKE & PARKER. Sunbeam Car. Refitting nature, dynamo shield, tightening up bracket. Pt GRANT. No 16 Cpl. O ORLIN. Refitting wheels Pt GRANT. Store lorry, making petty barrier for iron steel. Recopy Workshop lorry. Repairing switch board Pt KNIGHTLEY. Staff Workshops staff to Enlis at PERNAY. No 1 SECTION. Amb No 1. One journey to GOSNAY. Amb Nos 2, 3 & 6. One journey to NOEUX-LES-MINES. Amb. No 4. One journey to VAUDRICOURT. Amb No 5. One journey to BETHUNE. Amb No 7. Two journeys from HOUCHIN to HESDIGNEUL.	
HESDIGNEUL			No 2 SECTION. Amb. No 14. Journeys to CHOCQUES, & FOUQUIERES, & two to GOSNAY.	
VAUDRICOURT			No 3 SECTION. Coll. Collecting & Evacuating Amb. No 15, 32 mls; No 16, 16 mls; No 17 (in workshops);	
NOEUX-LES-MINES			No 18, 3 nuls; No 19, 10 nuls; No 20, 20 nuls; No 21, 46 nuls. B Edn Jn. VF R.A.C.	

Army Form C. 2118

WAR DIARY
or
INTELLIGENCE SUMMARY
(Erase heading not required.)

15th Divl [MT?]

Place	Date	Hour	Summary of Events and Information	Remarks and references to Appendices
HESDIGNEUL	25/8/15	Wed.	WORKSHOP. No 16 Wolseley Grinding in valves. Pte LAKE & ROSE. Wolseley Car No M9414 Major Brown A.O.D. Tuning up Engine, carburetter, magneto & examining car. Staff Sergt CUTLER & Pte ALLTHORPE. Sunbeam Car. Grinding in valves. Pte GRANT & PARKER. 15th Divl Laundry. Repairing door & fitting locks. Cpl CHAMBERLIN & Pte BARFIELD. Shaking Sanitary blankets. Pte KNIGHTLEY & PARKER. Staff workshop staff went to Baths at BRUAY.	Do. [in the?] Field
HESDIGNEUL			No 1 SECTION. Amb No 1. One journey to LILLERS. Amb Nos 2,3,& 4. Journey to NOEUX-LES-MINES.	"
VAUDRICOURT			Amb Nos 2, 3 & 6. Journey to NOEUX-LES-MINES. Amb No 3. Journey to CHOCQUES. Amb. No 7. Two Journeys from HOUCHIN to HESDIGNEUL.	
NOEUX-LES-MINES			No 2 SECTION. Amb. No 13. Journey to LILLERS. Amb. No 14. Journey to GOSNAY. No 3 SECTION. Collecting & evacuating. Amb. No 15. 8 cals; No 16. 9cals; No 17. 40cals; No 18. 8cals; No 19. 56cals; No 20, 24 cals; No 21, 10 cals.	B.E.W. [Ltn?] Lt/Col ADSS
HESDIGNEUL	26/8/15	Thurs.	WORKSHOP. Sunbeam Car. Grinding in valves & adjusting tappets. Pte LAKE & PARKER. Wolseley car (Major Brown I.A.M). Tuning & timing magneto, shaft drive, relining footbrake, adjusting side brake, washing out clutch, oiling springs to car. S. Sergt CUTLER, Pte LAKE, BARFIELD, ALLTHORPE, GRANT, & ROSE. Wolseley No 10/(15V cacalin?) Refixing spring in valves. Ptes RATCLIFFE & PARKER.	

Army Form C. 2118.

WAR DIARY
or
INTELLIGENCE SUMMARY.
(Erase heading not required.)

Instructions regarding War Diaries and Intelligence Summaries are contained in F. S. Regs., Part II. and the Staff Manual respectively. Title pages will be prepared in manuscript.

Place	Date	Hour	Summary of Events and Information	Remarks and references to Appendices
HESDIGNEUL	26/8/15	Thurs.	WORKSHOP (cont.) Making clips to carry picks & shovels. Lce Cpl PRINCE & Pte CLAYTON. Jnd to H.Q. ST. OMER to purchase stores.	Driesfeld
HESDIGNEUL &			No 1 SECTION. Amb. No 5. Journeys to HOUCHIN & VAUDRICOURT. Amb No 2, 3 & 6 Journeys to NOEUX-LES-MINES. Amb. No 4. Journeys to LABEUVRIERE & VAUDRICOURT. Amb. No 7. Journey from HOUCHIN to HESDIGNEUL.	"
LABEUVRIERE			All Ambulances (Nos 1-7) moved from HESDIGNEUL to LABEUVRIERE to new station. Amb Nos 1 & 5 return journeys between HESDIGNEUL & LABEUVRIERE. Engaged in moving. Amb No 2, 3 & 6 one journey to NOEUX-LES-MINES.	
VAUDRICOURT			No 2 SECTION. Amb. No 8. Journey to COSNAY. Amb. No 10 Journey to LILLERS. Amb No 11. MAZINGARBE. Amb. No R. Road work. Amb. No 13 Journey to BETHUNE. Amb. No 14 FOUQUIERES.	"
			No 3 SECTION. Collecting & Evacuating. Amb. No 15, 14 mls; Amb. No 16, 10 mls; Amb No 17, 12 mls; Amb No 18, 20 mls; Amb No 19, 13 mls; Amb No 20, 20 mls; Amb No 21, 20 mls.	"
				B & Lt U.N.C.
HESDIGNEUL	27/8/15		WORKSHOP Holesby Cpl (Major BROWN A.O.D.) fitting radiator stays on S.Sgt CUTLER, Pte ALLTHORPE. O Pte LAKE. No 28 Motorly finding valves Pte RATCLIFFE & PARKER Re-tying car S.Sgt CUTLER. Lce 14 Ford (Lce 2 Austin) fitting new spring eye bolt Pte POPE. No 19 Wolseley 3 Seat. Taking down rear spring clips & nutting new retainers. Ptes PARKER & CLAYTON.	"

Army Form C. 2118.

WAR DIARY
or
INTELLIGENCE SUMMARY.
(Erase heading not required.)

15th Divnl S.A.A.C.

Instructions regarding War Diaries and Intelligence Summaries are contained in F. S. Regs., Part II. and the Staff Manual respectively. Title pages will be prepared in manuscript.

Place	Date	Hour	Summary of Events and Information	Remarks and references to Appendices
HESDIGNEUL	27/8/15	Fri	WORKSHOP (cont'd) Workshop forgot tools & filling sand bags for Pte CLAYTON'S ROSE. I went to LILLERS to a report. Set to D.D. of M.S. & Army. Both factories busy. Known everything recovering and sent on going over difficulties or detail of repair with KARRIER lorry & 4 push lorry.	Details filed.
LABUISSIERE			No.1 SECTION. Auto Nos. 2,3,7,8. Ten journeys to NOEUX-LES-MINES. Amb. No.7. One journey to HESDIGNEUL & on to HOUCHIN.	4
VAUDRICOURT.			Amb No.7. One journey to HESDIGNEUL & on to ST OMER. No.2 SECTION Autos No's 10,13,º14 Journeys to MAZINGARBE; Amb No.13. Journey to FOUQUIERES - LABUISSIERE; Amb No.14. Journeys to BETHUNE & NOEUX-LES-MINES.	
NOEUX-LES-MINES			No.3 SECTION. Collecting Evacuating. Amb No.15. 8 miles; Amb No.16, 4 miles; Amb No.14. 15 miles; Amb No.18. (At Workshop) Amb No.19. 12 mls (to Workshop). Amb No.20. 20 miles; Amb No. 21. 24 miles.	
				B.S.Wilson Lt. R.A.M.C.
HESDIGNEUL	28/8/15	Sat	WORKSHOP No.19 Lorley (No 3 Sect) Securing filling near spring clip. Pte PARKER. No 5 Tra. Wilkey using rod retaining end. Pte CLAYTON-GRANT. I went to LILLERS. Reported to D.D. of M.S. & Army. Burke two clayton's rays, sent for spare spring & KARRIER Lorry, & arranged to make temporary repair their Lesior and carburetor. Spl belt to HESDIGNEUL.	

Army Form C. 2118.

WAR DIARY
or
INTELLIGENCE SUMMARY.
(Erase heading not required.)

15th Field (?)

Place	Date	Hour	Summary of Events and Information	Remarks and references to Appendices
LABEUVRIERE	28/8/15 Sat.		No 1 SECTION. Ambs Nos. 2, 3, & 6. Journey to NOEUX-LES-MINES. Amb Nos. 2, 8, & 7. Journey to VAUDRICOURT. Amb. No. 5. Two journeys to HESDIGNEUL. Amb. No. 4. Journey to MAZINGARBE. Amb. No. 6. Journey to HESDIGNEUL & on to BETHUNE. Amb No. 7. Journey to CHOCQUES. No 2 SECTION. Amb. No. 8. Journey to GOSNAY, district to LABUSSIERE. Amb. No. 9. Journey to MAZINGARBE. Amb. No. 11. Journey to VERQUIN, DROUIN, district. Amb. No. 13. Journey to BETHUNE. Amb. No. 14. Journey to LILLERS. No 3 SECTION. Amb. No 15, 46 mls; Amb. No 16, 12 mls; Amb. No 17, 10 mls; Amb. No 18, 128 miles; Amb. No. 19, 10 mls; Amb. No 20, 52 mls; Amb. No 21, 14 mls. Amb. No. 22, 18=79 returned to duty from workshop. During this amb fell tortoises except No 15 in this section were repaired by this drivers in the workshop at HESDIGNEUL.	Do 2/6 7/6 ?-?-?-? ?-?-?-? " "
			B.E.L.T. L.H.W.C.	
HESDIGNEUL	29/8/15 Sun.		WORKSHOP Sunbeam Car (Workshop Ser.D) Taking down front springs, fitting mudguardsprings. Taking down rear springs. Pte. GRANT & RATCLIFFE. Making mudguard clips. Pte. CLAYTON & HARDY. Harrier lorry (Workshop Ser.D) Repairing side brake rattle & fitting spain bolts. Pte L.A.K.I.	"
LABEUVRIERE			No 1 SECTION. Amb. No 1. Journey to HESDIGNEUL. Amb. No. 2, 3, & 6. Two journeys to NOEUX-LES-MINES. Amb No 4.	"

2353 Wt. W3544/1454 700,000 5/15 D. D. & L. A.D.S.S. Forms/C.2116.

Army Form C. 2118.

WAR DIARY
or
INTELLIGENCE SUMMARY.
(Erase heading not required.)

15th Disol F Amb U.

Place	Date	Hour	Summary of Events and Information	Remarks and references to Appendices
LABEUVRIERE	29/8/15 Sun.		No 1 SECTION (cont'd). Amb No 4. Journey to BROUAY. Amb No 5. Two journeys to HESDIGNEUL. Amb No 7. D.A.E.I Field	
			Journey to GOSNAY.	
VAUDRICOURT.			No 2 SECTION. Amb No 9. Journey to LILLERS. Amb No 12. Journey to LABUISSIERE & district. Amb No 13.	"
			Journey to LABUISSIERE, VAUDRICOURT & BETHUNE.	
NOEUX-LES-MINES.			No 3 SECTION. Collecting & evacuating. Amb No 16. 16 inds; Amb No 19, 18 inds; Amb No 20, 16 inds;	"
			Amb No 21, 18 inds.	
				Bleuth. E.F.A.C.
HESDIGNEUL	30/8/15 Mon.		WORKSHOP. Taking down new springs, making new leaf. Pte GRANT, RATCLIFFE, CLAYTON & HARDY.	"
			Ford No 20. (No 3 sect.) Fitting new horn. Sgt BARKER. Buick (old) (No 5 sect) taking out engine and	
			dismantling same. Ptes PARKER & LAKE.	
LABEUVRIERE			No 1 SECTION. Amb No 1. Journey to VAUDRICOURT. Amb No 2 & 6. Two journeys to NOEUX-LES-MINES.	"
			Amb No. 2,3 & 6. Journey to NOEUX-LES-MINES. Amb No 3. Journey to HESDIGNEUL & NOEUX-LES-MINES.	"
			Amb No 5. Journey to HESDIGNEUL. Amb No 6. Journey to LILLERS & LAPUGNOY. Amb No 7. Two	
			Journeys to CHOCQUES & Journey to ARQUE, VERQUIN & GOSNAY.	
VAUDRICOURT.			No 2 SECTION. Amb No 11. Journey to LILLERS & district. Amb No 13. Journey to BURNES. Amb No 14. Journey to	"
			LABEUVRIERE, MAZINGARBE, HESDIGNEUL and CHOCQUES.	

Army Form C. 2118.

WAR DIARY
or
INTELLIGENCE SUMMARY.
(Erase heading not required.)

15th Divl. Sig. Co. R.E.

Instructions regarding War Diaries and Intelligence Summaries are contained in F. S. Regs., Part II. and the Staff Manual respectively. Title pages will be prepared in manuscript.

Place	Date	Hour	Summary of Events and Information	Remarks and references to Appendices
NOEUX-LES-MINES	30/8/15	Mor	No 3 SECTION. Collecting + connecting. Amb No 15, 8 mls; Amb No 19, 16 mls; Amb No 20, 18 mls; Amb No 18, 40 mls; Amb No 21, 24 mls.	Distr/15/11
HESDIGNEUL	31/8/15	Luis.	WORKSHOP Motor Cycle (No 3 seat) Overhauling engine, & turning new gudgeon pin. Pts Lake & Rose	Clerks ko
			15. Grinding in valves + cleaning magneto. S. Sergt. CUTLER, Sergt BARKER & Pt ALLTHORPE. Linsbean	B.E. Hutton Lt. V.L.C.
			Car (Workshop lid.) Making petrol new cover, & assembling. Pts GRANT, RATCLIFF, CLAYTON	
			& HARDY. Sunbeam No 3 (No 1 Sec) Taking down shaft & front. Fitting new centre pin. Pt LAKE.	
			Wolseley Lo 15/ Ln 3 Sec) Repairing camera shroud. CpC CHAMBERLIN & Pt BARFIELD	
LABEUVRIERE			No 1 SECTION. Amb No 1. Journeys to CHOCQUES, HESDIGNEUL, LAPUGNOY, BETHUNE. Amb No 1.	
			Journey to CHOCQUES, Hd Qrs & A.D.S., LILLERS, CHOCQUES, BETHUNE, LAPUGNOY, CHOCQUES.	
VAUDRICOURT			Amb No 3. Journey to VAUDRICOURT & HESDIGNEUL. Amb No 4, 5 & 7 Various journeys to NOEUX-LES-MINES.	
			No 2 SECTION. Amb No 10 Journey to Workshop at HESDIGNEUL. Amb No 11 Journey to NOEUX-LES-MINES. Amb No 12 Ambce to BROWNIN.	
			Amb No 13 Journey to BROWNIN, LABUSSIERE, & LABEUVRIERE. Amb No 14. Journey to HERMENEUVILLE & LABUSIERE.	
NOEUX-LES-MINES			No 3 SECTION. Collecting + evacuating. Amb 15 (at Workshop), Amb No 17, 9 mls; Amb No 18, 18 mls;	
			Amb No 20, 17 mls; Amb No 21, 24 miles.	B.E. Hutton Lt V.L.C.

August 1st Sunday.

WORKSHOP. Pte LAKE made & fitted petrol tank washers on Sunbeam car.

Pte RATCLIFFE altered valve grinders for No 2 section.

Pte GRANT checked tappet clearance & fitted new front spring clip bolt on No 13 Ford, (No 2 section)

Ptes GRANT & RATCLIFFE removed cylinder heads & cleaned pistons & cylinder head & ground in valves on Ford No 20 (No 3 section)

Pte KNIGHTLEY made 3 letter trays for A.D.M.S. office from old biscuit tins.

I visited No 2 & 3 Sections with L.S. Sergt CUTLER. Examined petrol used by No 2 section, about which a complaint had been made. Found small quantity of water & rust in same.

No 2 SECTION. No 8 Ambulance proceeded at 2 p.m. to LILLERS, returned 4.30 p.m.

No 1. SECTION. No 2 Ambulance proceeded to LABOUVRIERE at 2.5 p.m. returned to HESDIGNEUL at 3.0 p.m.

No 3. SECTION. Cars used for collecting from Brigade Aid Posts & evacuating from Advanced Dressing Stations to Field Dressing Hospital at NEUX-LES-MINES.

Cars stationed as under.

No 15 } WOLSELEY Stationed at LES BREBIS.
No 18 }   Advanced dressing station.

No 19 } WOLSELEY } Stationed at MAZINGARBE
No 20 } FORD   } Advanced Dressing Station.

No 16 }
No 17 } WOLSELEY } Stationed at NEUX-LES-MINES.
No 21. FORD.   } Field Dressing Hospital.

Aug 1st (Sunday) (Cont'd)
SECTION 3. (cont'd)

	Mileage	Patients
Amb. No 15	16	7
" " 16	8	nil.
" " 17	10	nil.
" " 18	12	4
" " 19	4	nil.
" " 20	20	4
" " 21	20	3.

Sgt. BOWLER i/c section

B E Sutton Lt A.S.C.
15th Div'n F.A. Wks.

Aug 2nd. (Monday)

WORKSHOP. FORD AMBULANCE. No 13. (No 46. Fd. Amb)
Removing cylinder heads, cleaning off deposit, grinding in valves & reassembling.
Started 9 a.m. Finished 12 noon. Sgt BARKER & Pte PARKER.
FORD. AMB. No 14. Removing cylinder heads, removing carbon deposit, grinding in valves & reassembling.
Started 9 a.m. Finished 12 noon. Ptes. RATCLIFFE & BARFIELD
FORD. AMB. No 20. Taking off cylinder heads, removing carbon deposit & grinding in valves. Started 9 a.m. Finished 12 noon.
Ptes LAKE & GRANT. (No 47. Field Amb)
FORD. AMB. No 6 (45th Fd. Amb) Taking off cylinder heads, removing carbon deposit, & grinding in valves, & assembling.
Started 2.30 p.m. Finished 5.0 p.m. Ptes RATCLIFFE & GRANT.
FORD. AMB No 7. (45th Fd. Amb). Taking off cylinder heads, removing carbon deposit, grinding in valves, & reassembling. Started 2.30 p.m. Finished 5.0 p.m. Ptes LAKE & PARKER.

No 1 SECTION. Amb. No 2 proceeded to LA BOUVRIERE at 2.5 p.m. returned at 3.10 p.m.
No 6. Amb. proceeded to BROUVIN, ALLOUAGNE, & LAPUGNOY at 9.15 a.m. returned 2.0 p.m.
No 7. Amb. proceeded to LA BOUVRIERE at 11.15 a.m. returned at 12.30 p.m.
No 1 Amb. proceeded to LILLERS at 2.30 p.m. returned at 5.0 p.m.
No 2. Amb. proceeded to ALLOUAGNE at 4.10 p.m. returned at 6.55 p.m.
NO 2 SECTION. No 8 Amb. proceeded to CHOCQUES at 11.30 a.m. Returned at 1.30 p.m.

Aug. 2nd Monday (Cont'd)

No 2 SECTION (cont'd) No 10 Amb. proceeded to ALLOUAGNE & HOUCHIN at 9.15 a.m. returned at 11.15 a.m. then to GOSNAY at 12 noon returned 1.45 p.m.
No 11 amb. proceeded to GOSNAY at 10.15 a.m. returned 11.15 a.m.
Nos 13 & 14 Ambs. proceeded to Workshop at HESDIGNEUL for repairs at 8.30 a.m. Returned at 2 p.m.
No 14. Amb. proceeded at 6 p.m. to GOSNAY returned at 7 p.m.

NO 3 SECTION. Evacuating Duties.

Amb. No	Mileage	Patients
Amb. 15	12	12
16	—	—
17	10	8
18	10	6
19	14	7
20	18	2
21	12	6

No 17. amb. broke gate change. Wired to Advanced M.T. Depot for replacement.

B E Sutton Lt R.A.S.C.

Aug. 3rd Tuesday

WORKSHOP No 1 Sunbeam. Repairing horn. 45th Fd. Amb.
Pte KNIGHTLEY.
Motor Cycle 146th Fd. Amb. Sgt FRANKLIN. Adjusting Front &
Back wheel bearings and Controls Ptes GRANT & LAKE
Making Sanitary Utensils for A.D.M.S. Pte KNIGHTLEY.

<u>No 1 SECTION</u> No 7 Amb. made 3 journeys to Dressing
Station at HOUCHIN. Stationed at HOUCHIN. Started 5.0 P.M.

<u>No 2 SECTION</u> No 14 Amb. proceeded to LILLERS
at 2.30 p.m. returned 5 p.m.

<u>No.1. SECTION.</u> Ambs. nos 4, 5 & 6 proceeded at
5.30 p.m. to NEUX-LES-MINES. Returned at 7.40 p.m.

<u>No 3. SECTION.</u> Evacuating duties.

Amb. no	Mileage	No of Patients
15	8	5
16	12	8
17	12	8
18	—	—
19	30	14
20	20	6
21	24	3

I went over with M.S. Sergt CUTLER to
LE BREBIS to examine no 17 WOLSELEY.
Examined cars at NEUX-LES-MINES.

B E Sutton Lt A.S.C.

Aug. 4th Wednesday.

WORKSHOP. Repairs to Motor Cycle, (47th Fd. Amb. Sgt BOWLER. Straightened footrest & mudguard. Started 9.30am Finished 11.30 a.m. Pte LAKE.

WOLSELEY No 17 (No 3 SECTION) Repaired change-speed gate Started 4 p.m. Finished 5 p.m. Ptes PARKER and GRANT.

Making Sanitary utensils for A.D.M.S. Pte KNIGHTLEY.

No 1 SECTION. Ambs. Nos. 4, 5 & 6 proceeded to NEUX-LES-MINES at 5.30 p.m. Returned at 7.40 p.m.

Ambs. Nos 4, 5 & 6 proceeded to NEUX-LES-MINES at 8.15 a.m. returned at 9.40 a.m.

Until further orders Ambces No 4, 5 & 6 (A sect) to proceed to NOEUX-LES-MINES daily at 9 a.m and 6 p.m.

Amb. No 6 proceeded to MAZINGARBE at 5 p.m returned at 6.40 p.m.

Ambces Nos 4 & 5 proceeded to NOEUX-LES-MINES at 5.20 p.m. Returned at 6.40 p.m.

No 2 SECTION. No Detail.

No 3 SECTION Evacuating Duties.

Amb No.	Mileage	No of Patients	Amb No	Mileage	No of Patients
15	13	2	19†	14	4
16	10	6	20	25	7
17*	10	—	21	30	—
18	10	3			

† Wing Slightly Bent.

* I went out on HARRIER Lorry with Lce. Cpl PRINCE & N.S.S. CUTLER. to NOEUX-LES-MINES to fetch in No 17 WOLSELEY. Worked on car at NOEUX-LES-MINES, & drove it to HESDIGNEUL, where workshop staff repaired it. Returned same day.

B.E.Sutton Lt. R.A.M.C.

30

Aug. 5th Thursday.
WORKSHOP Motor cycle No 2 SECTION (46th Fd.Amb)
Repaired exhaust valve lifter &c. 9.0 a.m - 10.30 a.m.
                              Pte LAKE.
No 1 SUNBEAM. Fitted new brush in magneto. 11.45 a.m -
12.0 noon. Pte ALDUS.
10H Singer Light Car. R.E. Signal Service (A.D.M.S. instructions)
   Repairs to crank-case 3.0 P.M. — 4.0 P.M. Pte PARKER.
No 1 SECTION. No 6. Amb. proceeded to MAZINGARBE at
  1.0 a.m. Returned 6.45 A.M.
   No 2. Amb. proceeded to LA PHILOSOPHE at 8.0 a.m.
    Returned 10.40 a.m.
   Nos 3.4.&5 Ambces proceeded to NOEUX-LES-MINES
  at 8.20 a.m. Returned at 9.50 a.m.
   No 7. Amb. left HOUCHIN at 12.15 p.m. proceeded to
   HESDIGNEUL and returned to HOUCHIN at 3.10 p.m.
   No 7 Amb. left HOUCHIN at 3.50 p.m. proceeded to Artillery
  Camp near HOUCHIN. Returned to Dressing Station HOUCHIN at 4.20 pm
   No 7 Amb. left HOUCHIN at 6.30 p.m. for HESDIGNEUL and
   returned to HOUCHIN at. 9.50 p.m.
   No 1 Amb. proceeded to HAZEBROUCK at 2 p.m. continued
   to ARKUE and returned at 6.45 p.m.
   No 2 Amb. proceeded to LILLERS at 11.45 a.m.
    returned at 4.0 p.m. to HESDIGNEUL.
   No 3 Amb. proceeded to HOUCHIN at 6.45 p.m.
    Returned at 7.30 p.m.
 No 2 SECTION. No 9 amb. proceeded to GOSNAY
 at 12 noon. Returned to VAUDRICOURT at 12.30 pm
   No 13. Amb. proceeded to CHOCQUES at 3.30 p.m.

Aug. 5th Thursday, (Cont'd)

No 2 SECTION (cont'd)
and returned to VAUDRICOURT at 4.30 p.m.
No 10 Amb. did local work (VAUDRICOURT district)
from 10 a.m. to 10.30 a.m.
No 13 Amb. punctured; repaired by driver.
All valves ground in, oil sumps drained, cleaned
& replenished, & gear boxes & differential cases
examined by drivers & 2nd drivers of this section.
No 3 SECTION. Evacuating Duties.

Amb. no.	Mileage	No of Patients	Amb. no.	Mileage	Patients
15	16	4	19	4	2 collecting
16	8	4	20	34	4
17	24	Officers' Trans.	21	40	Medical Stores
18	13	6			

No 1 SECTION (45th Field Amb) Motor Cycle damaged
by Cpl DYER of the R.A.M.C. while acting as
orderly to the A.D.M.S.

B E Sutton Lt A.S.C.

Aug. 6th (Friday)

WORKSHOP

No 10. SUNBEAM. (46th Fd. Amb) (No 2 SECTION). Repairs to Differential Case 3.0 p.m. to 4.30 p.m. Ptes GRANT & RATCLIFFE

MOTOR Cycle (No 3 section) Inner tube repaired 9.30 a.m to 10 a.m
Pte ALDUS.

Motor Cycle (No 2 Section) Adjusting valves & testing cycle 10 a.m - 11 a.m.
Lce Cpl PRINCE.

Making Sanitary Utensils for A.D.M.S. Pte KNIGHTLEY.

No 1. SECTION. Amb. Nos. 4, 5 & 6 proceeded to NOEUX-LES-MINES. at 8.20 a.m. returned to HESDIGNEUL at 9.15 a.m.

No 3 Amb. proceeded to NOEUX-LES-MINES at 10.50 a.m. and returned to HESDIGNEUL at 11.50 a.m. a.m.

No 4. Amb. proceeded to NOEUX-LES-MINES at 7.15 p.m. & returned at to HESDIGNEUL at 8.15 p.m.

No 7. Amb. proceeded from HOUCHIN at 12.0 noon for HESDIGNEUL and returned to HOUCHIN at 3.15 p.m.

No 7 Amb. left HOUCHIN at 7.0 p.m. for HESDIGNEUL, & returned to HOUCHIN at 9.55 p.m.

No 2 SECTION No 10 Amb. proceeded at 11.45 a.m. to GOSNAY, & returned to VAUDRICOURT at 12.15 p.m.

No 10 Amb. proceeded to Workshop for repairs at 3 p.m. & returned to VAUDRICOURT at 4.45 p.m.

No 13. Amb. proceeded to DRUVAIN at 3.30 p.m. & returned to VAUDRICOURT at 4.30 p.m.

No 3 SECTION Evacuating Duties.

No of Amb.	Mileage.	Patients	Remarks.
15	14	3	Collecting & evacuating
16	10	—	Sanitation Officer

Aug. 6th Friday (Cont'd)
No 3 SECTION (cont'd)

No of Amb.	Mileage	Patients	Remarks
17	—	—	
18	12	2	Evacuating
19	12	5	Collecting & evacuating
20	38	8	" " "
21	45	3	" " "

B.E. Sutton Lt. A.S.C.

Aug. 7th. 1915. Saturday.   34

WORKSHOP. WORKSHOP LORRY. Alteration to Lamp
     Bracket.   Pte GRANT
Making Sanitary Utensils. Ptes KNIGHTLEY & PARKER.
NO 1 SECTION. Ambs nos. 4, 5 & 6 proceeded to
NOEUX-LES-MINES at 8.30 a.m. & returned to
HESDIGNEUL at 9.45 a.m.
Amb. No 6. proceeded to VAUDRICOURT at 10.0 A.m.
 & returned to HESDIGNEUL at 11.15 a.m.
Amb. No. 7. did local work at HOUCHIN from 6.50 a.m. to 7.15.a.m.
Ambs Nos 4, 5 & 6 proceeded to NOEUX-LES-MINES at 6.20 p.m.
 & returned to HESDIGNEUL at 9.10 p.m.
Amb. no 7. proceeded from HOUCHIN at 11.45 a.m. to
HESDIGNEUL and returned to HOUCHIN at 3.10 p.m.
NO. 2. SECTION. Amb. No 11. proceeded to CHOCQUES at
 8.15 a.m. & returned to VAUDRICOURT at 9.35 a.m.
Amb. no 13. proceeded to GOSNAY & district at 12.15 p.m. &
 returned to VAUDRICOURT at 1.15 p.m, then to DRUVAIN
 at 2.45 p.m returning at 3.30 p.m.
Amb. No 14 proceeded to CHOCQUES at 7 a.m. returning
 to VAUDRICOURT at 10 a.m. then to GOSNAY at 2.40 p.m.
 returning at 4 p.m.
M.C. Messenger work.
No 3 SECTION. Evacuating Duties
  No of Amb.   Mileage.   Patients   Remarks
    15   8   5   Evacuating
    16   No detail
    17   no detail.
    18   16   7   Collecting & evacuating

Aug 7th (Contd) Saturday.

No 3 SECTION (contd)

No of Car	Mileage	Patients	Remarks
19	28	4	Collecting and evacuating.
20	39	3	Collecting and evacuating.
21	28	1	Collecting and evacuating.

I went to AIRE in the morning to report to MAJOR McLEOD. (D.A.D.Y.)

B E Sutton Lt A.S.C.
15th Div. T.A & S.C.

Aug 7th (Contd)

No 1 SECTION. No 1 Amb. proceeded to GOSNAY at 3.10 p.m. and returned to HESDIGNEUL at 3.45 p.m.
  No 3 Amb. proceeded to BRUAY at 4.40 p.m. returned to HESDIGNEUL at 6.40 P.M.
  No 2 Amb. proceeded to LILLERS at 2.50 p.m. returned to HESDIGNEUL at 4.30 p.m.

B E Sutton Lt A.S.C.

Aug. 8th. Sunday.   36

WORKSHOP   Making Sanitary Utensils for A.D.M.S.
Ptes. KNIGHTLEY and PARKER.
  Ford. No 20 (47th Fd. Amb.) Adjusting Speeds
  and clutch (12.0 noon - 2.30 p.m) SERGT BARKER
  and PTE ALTHORPE.
  Sunbeam No 3. (45th Field Ambulance) Taking down
  gear box & stripping same to rectify grease leakage.
  Started 10.30 a.m.   Ptes GRANT and LAKE.

No 1 SECTION. No 3 Amb. proceeded to GOSNAY at 9 A.M.
  then on to LABUISSIERE & returned to HESDIGNEUL
  at 10.20 a.m.
            No 2 Amb. proceeded to NOEUX-LES-MINES
  at 9.10 a.m. & returned to HESDIGNEUL at 11.0 A.M.
  Ambs Nos 4, 5 & 6 proceeded to NOEUX-LES-MINES at 8.30 a.m.
  & returned to HESDIGNEUL at 9.25 a.m.
  Amb. No 2 proceeded to CHOCQUES at 7.25 p.m. and
  returned to HESDIGNEUL at 8.25 p.m.
  Amb. No 1. proceeded to LABUISSIERE at 8.15 p.m. and
  returned to HESDIGNEUL at 8.45 p.m.
  Amb. No 7. left HOUCHIN at 7.15 p.m. for HESDIGNEUL
  and returned to HOUCHIN at 9.40 p.m.
  Amb. No. 6 proceeded to DROUVIN at 2.45 p.m. and returned
  to HESDIGNEUL at 4.0 p.m.

No 2 SECTION Amb. No 13. did local general duty near
  VAUDRICOURT from 8.45 a.m. to 3.15 p.m.
  Amb. No. 14 proceeded to DROUVIN & GOSNAY at 12 noon &
  returned to VAUDRICOURT at 1 P.M.
  Amb. No 14. proceed to GOSNAY at 1.15 p.m. and returned

Aug. 8th (Sunday) (Cont'd)

<u>No 2 SECTION</u> (Cont'd)

to VAUDRICOURT at 1.45 p.m.

Amb. No 14 proceeded to HOUCHIN at 5 p.m. returning to VAUDRICOURT at 7 p.m.

M/cycle, general work. Two new plugs fitted by workshop.

<u>No 3 SECTION.</u>   Evacuating duties.

Car No.	Mileage.	Patients	Remarks.
15	12	2	Collecting and evacuating.
16	10	—	Passenger service.
17	6	4	Collecting and evacuating.
18	8	1	Evacuating.
19	25	9	Evacuating.
20	50	5	Evacuating.
21	14	—	Medical Stores.

B E Sutton Lt A.S.C.

Aug. 9th 1915. (Monday) 38

WORKSHOP. No 3 Sunbeam (45th Fd. Amb.) Assembling gear-box & fitting same in chassis. Finished 12.0 noon. Ptes. GRANT and LAKE.
Repairing damaged Wolseley Radiator for Stores Ptes.
      KNIGHTLEY and PARKER.
Making Sanitary Utensils for A.D.M.S. Pte PARKER.

NO 1 SECTION. No 1. Amb. proceeded to DROUVIN & CHOCQUES at 9.50 a.m. Returned to HESDIGNEUL at 12.30 p.m.
Amb. No 3. proceeded to BETHUNE at 5.10 p.m. returned to HESDIGNEUL at 6.35 p.m.
Amb. No. 2. proceeded to ST. OMER at 2 p.m. and returned at 6.35 p.m.
Amb. No 6 proceeded to CHOCQUES at 7 p.m. and returned to HESDIGNEUL at 8.15 p.m.
Ambs. Nos. 4, 5 & 8 proceeded to NOEUX-LES-MINES at 8.45 a.m. returning to HESDIGNEUL at 9.45 a.m. also at 5.35 p.m. returning at 6.40 p.m.
Amb. No. 7. left HOUCHIN for HESDIGNEUL at 7.30 p.m. returning to HOUCHIN at 10.50 p.m.

NO 2. SECTION. Amb. NO 12. proceeded from DROUVIN to GOSNAY at 11.15 a.m. returning at 12.30 pm
Amb. No 13. proceeded to LILLERS at 2.10 p.m. returning to VAUDRICOURT at 4.45 p.m.
Amb. No 14. proceeded to GOSNAY at 12. noon, and returned to VAUDRICOURT at 1 P.M.
Amb. No 14. proceeded to GOSNAY at 3 p.m. returning to VAUDRICOURT at 4 p.m.
Amb. No 14 proceeded to BETUNE at 6 P.M. & returned to VAUDRICOURT at 8. P.M. with Medical Stores.

Aug. 9th Monday. (Contd)

No. SECTION. No. 13 Amb. proceeded to PHILOSOPHE at 6.30 A.M. returning to VAUDRICOURT at 8.30 a.m. No. 14. Amb. proceeded to DROUVIN and GOSNAY at 11.A.M. returning at 12 noon.

No. 3. SECTION. Evacuating Duties.

No of Car	Mileage	Patients	Remarks
15	8	3	Evacuating
16	—	—	—
17	10	—	Officer Passenger
18	8	5	Evacuating
19	16	5	Collecting & Evacuating
20	26	4	Collecting and Evacuating
21	24	—	Medical Stores

Unit Examined by Major HUTCHINSON, D.Dof.T. who reported favourably. Interviewed Col RAWNSLEY A.D.M.S. with reference to outside work being done in the workshops, use of motor cycles &c.

B. Sutton Lt. A.S.C.

15/7/14

15.A Division

15. F. Dirl: F.A.w.u.
rol: 3
Sepl. 15.

Army Form C. 2118

WAR DIARY
or
INTELLIGENCE SUMMARY.
(Erase heading not required.)

15th Div. Train & A.S.C. H.Q.

Instructions regarding War Diaries and Intelligence Summaries are contained in F. S. Regs., Part II. and the Staff Manual respectively. Title pages will be prepared in manuscript.

Place	Date	Hour	Summary of Events and Information	Remarks and references to Appendices
HESDIGNEUL	1/9/15	Wed.	WORKSHOP. Reissuing tops of (cookstoves) Stogey engines. Anti workshop engine fitting fan blades on flywheel. Motor Cycle (No 3 Sect) Overhauling engine, turning plug & springs. Ford No 20 (No 3 Sect) fitting new tires, fell washers on axle, straightening wheel & pipes.	Debit & Credit
LABUVRIERE	"	"	No.1. SECTION. Ambs No 4, 5 & 7. Two journeys to NOEUX-LES-MINES. Amb No 1. Journey to HESDIGNEUL & GOSNAY & to FOUQUEREUIL. Amb. No 6 Journey to DROUVIN. Amb. No 4. Journey to CHOCQUES.	"
VAUDRICOURT	"	"	No 2. SECTION. Amb No 8. No 9. Journey to LABUSSIERE. Amb. No 10. Journey to LABUSSIERE district. Amb No. 14. Journey to MAZINGARBE, FOUQUEREUIL district.	"
NOEUX-LES-MINES.	"	"	No 3. SECTION. Collecting Economy ft.h No. 15. 19 miles; No 16. 7 mls; No 19. 20 mls; No 20, 32 mls; No 21, 24 mls.	"
HESDIGNEUL.	2/9/15	Thurs.	WORKSHOP Sanitary section Kidney Pump. Repair	Ditto Ditto Ditto
HESDIGNEUL.	2/9/15	Thurs.	WORKSHOP Sanitary Sect. Repairing "Kidney" Pump. hylex (No 3 sect) Overhauling engine, fitting cam + frame. Chassis Workshop Engine, fitting blades on wheel. Half workshop went to Bath at BRUAY.	"
LABUVRIERE.	"	"	No 1 SECTION. Amb No 1 Journey to BETHUNE. No 1.13 Journey to LAPUGNOY. No. 3 Journey to VAUDRICOURT & HESDIGNEUL Ambs No 3, 4, 5 & 7 Two journeys to NOEUX-LES-MINES. No 3 Journey to CHOCQUES. No 4. No 6 Journey to BRUAY & FOUQUEREUIL.	"
VAUDRICOURT.	"	"	No 2 SECTION Amb No. 8 Journey to MAZINGARBE, NOEUX-LES-MINES, LILLERS. No 9 Lestrembles. No 12 Journey to BRUAY. No 12 Journey to LAPUGNY. No 13 Journey to MAZINGARBE 9 to Two Journey to LABEUVRIERE & LAPUGNY. No 14. Journey to HESDIGNEUL & LABEUVRIERE, LABEUVRIERE, & VERQUIN, to BETHUNE. No. 14. Journey to HESDIGNEUL & LABEUVRIERE.	"

WAR DIARY or INTELLIGENCE SUMMARY

Army Form C. 2118.

5th Res. M.A.S.C.

Place	Date	Hour	Summary of Events and Information	Remarks and references to Appendices
NOEUX-LES-MINES	2/9/15	Thurs	No 1a) No 3 SECTION Collecting Evacuating. Amb No 15, 16 aub; No 17, 29 aub; No 18, 28 aub; No 20, 30 aub; No 21, 16 aub. Do E 19 Field Workshop. Half workshop to baths at BROUAY. B.Hutton Lt/Col A.S.C.	
HESDIGNEUL	3/9/15	Fri'd	WORKSHOP. Motor Cycle (No 3 set) Lillipetpin & carburette. 2 coming out 47th Bn N.O.D. Lorry out of diet at VAUDRICOURT. Very wet day made work at workshops almost impossible.	
LABEUVRIERE			No 1 SECTION. Amb. No 1. Journey to HESDIGNEUL. Amb No 2. Journey to HESDIGNEUL G NOEUX-LES-MINES & LAPUGNOY. Amb. No 3. Journey to VAUDRICOURT. Amb No 4. Journey to CHOCQUES. Amb No 5. & 6. Journey to NOEUX-LES-MINES. Amb No 4, 5, & 7. Journey to NOEUX-LES-MINES. Amb No 11. Journey to LILLERS. No 2 SECTION. Amb Nos 9 & 11 Journey to LABEUVRIERE. Amb No 10. Journey to LAPUGNOY & LABEUVRIERE. Amb No 11. Journey to LILLERS. Amb No 14. Journey to DROUVIN & district.	
NOEUX-LES-MINES			No 3 SECTION. Collecting & evacuating. Amb No 15. 66 aub; Amb No 16. 76 aub; Amb No 18. 38 aub; Amb No 20. 30 aub; Ambl No 21. 44 aub. B.Hutton Lt/Col A.S.C.	
HESDIGNEUL	4/9/15	Sat	WORKSHOP. Motor Cycle (No 3 set.) Overhauling. Half Workshops went to the Bath at BROUAY.	
LABEUVRIERE			No 1 SECTION Amb No 1, 4, 5, 7. Less Journeys to NOEUX-LES-MINES. Amb No 1. Journey to NOEUX-LES-MINES, MAZINGARBE & LABEUVRIERE. Amb No 2. Journey to HESDIGNEUL. Amb No 3. Journey to PHILOSOPHE. Amb No 1 & 4. 1. Journey to HESDIGNEUL. Amb No 2. Journey to VAUDRICOURT & BETHUNE. Amb No 3. Journey to VAUDRICOURT & BETHUNE. Journey to LILLERS. Amb Nos. 1, 2, 3 & 4. Journey to NOEUX-LES-MINES.	
VAUDRICOURT			No 2 SECTION. Amb No 13. Journey to BETHUNE, PHILOSOPHE & district, VAUDRICOURT, BETHUNE. Amb No 14. Journey to PHILOSOPHE & LABEUVRIERE.	
NOEUX-LES-MINES			No 3 SECTION. Collecting & evacuating. Amb No 15, 32 aub; Amb No 18, 18 aub; Amb No 20, 30 aub; Amb No 21, 21 aub. B.Hutton Lt/Col A.S.C.	

WAR DIARY
or
INTELLIGENCE SUMMARY.
(Erase heading not required.)

Army Form C. 2118.

15th Div. T.A.S.C.

Place	Date	Hour	Summary of Events and Information	Remarks and references to Appendices
HESDIGNEUL	5/9/15	Sun.	WORKSHOP. Motorly No 15 (tho 3 seats). Repairing Jack, Pump, tyres. I went to NOEUX-LES-MINES to inspect Wolseley vehicles of 47th F.A. Amb. Motor Cycles No 3 (seal) in workshop.	
LABEUVRIERE			No 1 SECTION. Ambs Nos 4 & 5 Lv. journey. Nos 6 & 7. One journey to NOEUX-LES-MINES. Ambs No 1B 3 & 7, moved to NOEUX-LES-MINES.	
NOEUX-LES-MINES			Amb. No 2. One journey to NOEUX-LES-MINES from LABEUVRIERE Return. Amb. No 1 Journey to HESDIGNEUL, thence No 5 Journey to MAZINGARBE.	
VAUDRICOURT.			Amb No 3. Journey to MAZINGARBE.	
			No 2 SECTION. Amb. No 8 & 14. Journey to PHILOSOPHE. Amb. No 10. Journey to DROUIN & LABEUVRIERE. Ambs Nos 11, 12 & 14. Journey from	
			LABEUVRIERE to VAUDRICOURT. Ambs No 13 & 14. Journey to HESDIGNEUL.	
			No 3 SECTION. Activity Reconnoitring. Amb. No 15, 22 mls, Amb No 17, 8 mls, Amb No 20, 32 mls, Amb No 21, 40 mls. Bell the N.A.S.C.	
NOEUX-LES-MINES	6/9/15	Mon.	WORKSHOP. No 2 Sunbeam. Repairing Damaged mudguard. Ford No 14 (tho 2 seat) Testing 2 new tyres, repairing generator. Ford No 13	
HESDIGNEUL			(tho 2 seats) Repairing Lamp. No 12 Sunbeam (tho 2 seat) Repairing Petal cycle. Type Enlarge plain, making packs for lifts etc. workshops	
NOEUX-LES-MINES			No 1 SECTION. Amb No 2. Ian journeys 9 Ambs Nos 3 & 7. One journey to LABEUVRIERE. Amb No 4. Journey to LABEUVRIERE ?	
			LAPUGNOY. Amb No 3. Journey to MAZINGARBE. Amb No 5 Journey to FOUQUEREUIL. Amb No 6 Journey from LABEUVRIERE to NOEUX-LES-MINES.	
LABEUVRIERE.			Amb No 6. Journey to HESDIGNEUL. NOEUX-LES-MINES. Amb No 5 Journey to LAPUGNOY. Amb No 6 Journey to LAPUGNOY & LILLERS.	
			Amb No 5 Journey to NOEUX-LES-MINES. Amb No 1 journey from NOEUX-LES-MINES to LABEUVRIERE. Ambs 1,2,3,4 & 6 journey to HESDIGNEUL	
			No 2 SECTION. Ambs. hired at outskirts of theatre & the background & Col Evans Amb No 8 & 13 Journey to NOEUX-LES-MINES.	
VAUDRICOURT.			Ambs Nos 8 & 14 Journey to LILLERS. Amb No 10. Journey to PHILOSOPHE. Amb No 19 Journey to LAPUGNOY. Amb No 8 Journey to LABEUVRIERE	

2353 Wt. W3544/7454 700,000 5/15 D. D. & L. A.D.S.S. Forms/C.2118.

WAR DIARY
or
INTELLIGENCE SUMMARY

Army Form C. 2118

15th Div'l T.T.& Co. A.

Place	Date	Hour	Summary of Events and Information	Remarks and references to Appendices
NOEUX-LES-MINES	6/9/15	Even.	No 3 SECTION. Collecting & evacuating. Amb. No 15, 6 miles; Amb. No 16, 36 miles; Amb. No 20, 36 miles; A.S. No 21, 27 miles.	Detail Filed. B.Batta. S.A.S.C.
HESDIGNEUL	7/9/15	Even.	WORKSHOP. Daimler Lorry. (32 Sanitary bodies) making fitting for seats to A.D.M.S. instructions. Sunbeam lorry 2. (No 1 Sect.) Lightning readjusted tripods to workshops. Repairing fittings. Harvier Lorry Painting car & towing cover. Workshop making both carrier Harrier. Making cover for grease. Ambulances B.S. Etto & numbered.	"
LABEUVRIERE			No 1 SECTION. Amb No 6. Journey to HESDIGNEUL, VAUDRICOURT, VAUDRICOURT ad NOEUX-LES-MINES. Amb No 5. Journey to LILLERS to NOEUX-LES-MINES.	"
VAUDRICOURT			No 2 SECTION. Amb No 9. Journey to PHILOSOPHE. Amb No 12. Journey to MAZINGARBE. Amb No 13. Journey to BOSNAY, CHOCQUES, LILLERS to BETHUNE & BOSNAY. Amb No 14. Journey to LABEUVRIERE, MAZINGARBE, & RURT.	"
NOEUX-LES-MINES			No 3 SECTION. Auto Collectly & evacuating. Amb No 15, 21 miles; Amb No 21, 28 mls.	B.Batta. S.A.S.C.
HESDIGNEUL	8/9/15	8rd	WORKSHOP. Repg f fittings for tripod. Daimler Sanitary lorry. Making fitting seats in body. Harvier Lorry. Repairing camp & making grease cover for tasring. Half Workshop went to Cathedral at BRUAY.	"
LABEUVRIERE			No 1 SECTION. Amb No 6. Journey to BRUAY, HESDIGNEUL, ELAPUMOI, & NOEUX-LES-MINES. Amb No 5. Journey to NOEUX-LES-MINES to ST.OMER. Amb No 4. Journey to BOSNAY. Amb No 39 4. Journey from NOEUX-LES-MINES to	"

WAR DIARY or INTELLIGENCE SUMMARY

Army Form C. 2118

5th Div. T.A&M.U.

Place	Date	Hour	Summary of Events and Information	Remarks and references to Appendices
LABEUVRIERE	8/9/15	Wed.	**No 1 SECTION (cont)** LABEUVRIERE No 2.3	Det. 3rd Std
VAUDRICOURT	8/9/15	—	No 2 SECTION. Ambs Nos. 8,10,11,12 & 14 to workshops for frain tg. Amb No 9 & 11 Journey to MAZINGARBE. Amb No 9 Journey to LABEUVRIERE. Amb No 12 & 14 Journey to PHILOSOPHE. Amb No 13 Journey to NOEUX-LES-MINES. Amb No 4 Journey to ST. OMER.	"
NOEUX-LES-MINES			No 3 SECTION. Colliery Evacuating. Amb No 15, 24 miles; Amb No 11, 24 mls; Amb No 20, 22 mls; Amb No 21, 44 miles B.8 litres LtAMC	"
HESDIGNEUL	9/9/15	Thurs	WORKSHOP Motor cycle (No 3 Section) hub& flywheel key. Hasser lorry, leaking petrol tank, fitting new clutch thrust race, [illeg] pipes. Sunbeam No 12 (No 2 section) shaking down rear spring relieving oil leakage from rear axle. Daimler lorry (32 Sanitary Section) taking off cylinder heads & cleaning off carbon deposit.	"
LABEUVRIERE	9/9/15	Thurs	No 1 SECTION Amb No 3. Journey to NOEUX-LES-MINES. Amb No 4. Journey to NOEUX-LES-MINES. Amb No 6. Journey to HESDIGNEUL & then to BETHUNE & NOEUX-LES-MINES. Amb No 7. Journey to LABEUVRIERE.	"
NOEUX-LES-MINES				
VAUDRICOURT			No 2 SECTION. Ambs No 10 & 13 Journeys to PHILOSOPHE. Amb No 8. Journey to LILLERS. Amb No 12. Journey to workshops. at HESDIGNEUL. Amb No 13 Journey to BETHUNE.	"
NOEUX-LES-MINES			No 3 SECTION. Colliery Evacuating. Amb No 15, 14 mls; Amb No 9, 20 mls; Amb No 20, 30 mls; Amb No 21, 22 mls B.8 litres LtAMC	"

Army Form C. 2118

WAR DIARY
or
INTELLIGENCE SUMMARY.
(Erase heading not required.)

15th Div. Trab.
B.tt. H.M.A.C.

Instructions regarding War Diaries and Intelligence Summaries are contained in F. S. Regs., Part II. and the Staff Manual respectively. Title pages will be prepared in manuscript.

Place	Date	Hour	Summary of Events and Information	Remarks and references to Appendices
HESDIGNEUL	10/9/15	7 A.M.	WORKSHOP. Sunbeam No.5. (Mec. Seal.) Fitting new clutch leather, examining various points, adjusting tappets. Detailed for testing car. Daimler Lorry. (21 Sanitary Sect.) Loose cylinder, taking string of ear, fitting seats, finishing same. Mo. Section. Repairing spanner. Half workshop on detail at BRUAY.	
LABEUVRIERE			No.1 SECTION. Amb. No 6 two journeys to 4 Cas. journey to NOEUX-LES-MINES. Amb. No. 5 No 6 journeys.	
NOEUX-LES-MINES			HESDIGNEUL. Amb. No. 3. Journey to MAZINGARBE. Amb. No. 9. Journey to LABEUVRIERE.	
VAUDRICOURT			No.2 SECTION. Amb. Nos. 11 & 14 Journeys to PHILOSOPHE. Amb No. 12 Journey to NOEUX-LES-MINES and HAILLICOURT. Amb No. 14. Journey to NOEUX-LES-MINES & LAPUGNOY.	
NOEUX-LES-MINES			No.3 SECTION. C.M.a.C. Journey. Amb No. 15. 28 mls. ; Amb. No. 19. 28 mls. ; Amb. No 21. 46 mls. B.Batt. L.H.P.C.	
HESDIGNEUL.	11/9/15	Sed.	WORKSHOP. Daimler Lorry Sanitary Section checking spare parts of some. Lucken Car. Repairing head lamp connection. Journey to AIRE to rejoint to take returns to D.D.G.A.T. No Army	
LABEUVRIERE			No.1 SECTION. Amb. Nos. 4 & 6. Journey to NOEUX-LES-MINES. Amb. No. 5. Journey to HESDIGNEUL & LILLERS. Amb. No. 5 Journey to LAPUGNOY.	
VAUDRICOURT			No.2 SECTION. Amb. No. 13. two journeys & Amb. No. 14. Cas. Journey to HESDIGNEUL & DROUVIN. Amb No. 13. Journey to NOEUX-LES-MINES & Amb. No. 14. Journey to PHILOSOPHE.	
NOEUX-LES-MINES			No. 3. SECTION. Cleaning & Greasing. Amb. No. 15. 20 mls ; Amb. No. 15. 10 mls ; Amb. No. 20. 6 mls ; Amb. No. 21. 38 mls. B. Batt. LHFAC	

Army Form C. 2118

WAR DIARY
or
INTELLIGENCE SUMMARY.

(Erase heading not required.) 15th Div'l M.T. Coy & Workshops, Lorette Field, M.E.F.

Instructions regarding War Diaries and Intelligence Summaries are contained in F.S. Regs., Part II. and the Staff Manual respectively. Title pages will be prepared in manuscript.

Place	Date	Hour	Summary of Events and Information	Remarks and references to Appendices
HESDIGNEUL	12/9/15	Sun	WORKSHOP. No Workshop Detail	
LABEUVRIERE			No 1 SECTION. Amb No 5. Two journeys & Amb No 3. Gun Journey to HESDIGNEUL. Amb. No 6. Journey to GOSNAY.	Detailed
			HESDIGNEUL. 9 Ambs LAPUGNOY. Amb. No 4 Journey to BETHUNE.	
NOEUX-LES-MINES.			Amb No 2. Journey to LABEUVRIERE.	
VAUDRICOURT.			No 2 SECTION. Amb No 9. Journey to LABOURNE, PHILOSOPHE Amb. Col. 1/6/10 Journey to LILLERS. No 8. No 14 Journey to LAPUGNOY.	
			Amb No 13. Journey to PHILOSOPHE. Amb. No 14. Journey to AUCHEL & GOSNAY.	
NOEUX-LES-MINES.			No 3 SECTION Allery Heavily; Amb No 15. 42 mls; Amb. No 17. 40 mls; Amb. No 18. 20 mls; Amb. No 19. 54 mls. Amb. No 20. 8 miles Amb No 21. 10 miles	B.Butler Lt.A.S.C.
HESDIGNEUL.	13/9/15.	Mon.	WORKSHOP. Harvicoating, taking down valleys, pond fyling, bringing up water &c. Standing dead kind.	
LABEUVRIERE.			No 1 SECTION. Amb. No. 6. Journey to VAUDRICOURT. Amb. No 5 & 6.	
			Journey to NOEUX-LES-MINES	
VAUDRICOURT.			No 2 SECTION. Amb. No 8. Journey to HESDIGNEUL & LILLERS. Amb. No. 9. Journey to LAPUGNOY. Amb No. 10 Journey to LAPUGNOY. Amb No 16. Mass.	
			Journey to MAZINGARBE. Amb. No 12 Journey to PHILOSOPHE. Amb. No 33. Journey to LABEUVRIERE, BETHUNE & LAPUGNOY. Amb No 14. Journey to ARQUES. Staying there.	
NOEUX-LES-MINE.			No 3 SECTION. Collecting generally. Amb No 15. 2 orbs, Amb. No 16. 30 mls; Amb No 17. 32 mls, Amb. No 18. 42 mls. Amb. No 20. 10 mls; Amb No 21. 38 mls.	B.Butler Lt.A.S.C.

WAR DIARY
or
INTELLIGENCE SUMMARY.

(Erase heading not required.) 15th D.S.A. Field Ambulance Wakefield field C.C.S.

Army Form C. 2118

Place	Date	Hour	Summary of Events and Information	Remarks and references to Appendices
HESDIGNEUL	14/9/15	—	WORKSHOP. No 1 Sunbeam Lorry 2 Section fitting new rear spring centre bolt. Sunbeam No 2 (Chester) fitting new packing pieces to rear spring. Ford No 21 (Chrysler) fitting new shock absorbers to back wheel chassis. Sunbeam car. Repairing footboards & rear seat covering. Starter lever, fixing of lifting side door screen. Inspected 4 (?) Ford Ambs. at back at BRUAY.	Ditto to? Field
			NOEUX-LES-MINES, MAZINGARBE, and part of 4.5 at NOEUX-LES-MINES staff monthly t Batt at BRUAY.	
LABEUVRIERE			No 1 SECTION. Amb No 6. Journey to NOEUX-LES-MINES. Amb No 3. Journey to LABUSSIERE.	
NOEUX-LES-MINES			Amb No 4 Journey to BETHUNE. ____ Amb No 2. Journey to HESDIGNEUL's MAZINGARBE.	
VAUDRICOURT			No 2 SECTION. Amb No 11 Journey to Intertal pd HESDIGNEUL & LAPUG No 18 + EEQUIN Amb No 12 Journey to VERQUIN Amb No 13 Journey	
			to Journey to PHILOSOPHE on to BETHUNE. Amb No 14. Journey from RQUES & St OMER's & return.	
NOEUX-LES-MINES			No 3 SECTION. Collecting & evacuating Watto 15, 24 mby, Amb No 16, 26 mby, Amb No 17, 24 mby Amb No 20. 56 mly Amb No 21, 44 Lt Batt & HAC.	
HESDIGNEUL	15/9/15	B.d.	WORKSHOP. Motor cycle (No 2 Sect) V & Journey carrier, mispelling crupshaft & ring, Carries voyant & Weight M707. wind screen. Sunbeam Lo 4 (Chr.Sect) Changing turn. Rear axle (No 2 sect). Removing flywheel, fitting & removing same. Darracq	
			to NOEUX-LES-MINES to see O.C. of 47 (?)Lt? H Amb. about repairs to ambulances.	
LABEUVRIERE			No 1 SECTION. Amb No 5 Journey to HESDIGNEUL. Amb No 6, 5+8 Journeys to NOEUX-LES-MINES. Amb No 1, Journeys to BETHUNE	
			and LILLERS. Amb No 4 Journey to VAUDRICOURT.	
NOEUX-LES-MINES			Amb No 7 Journey to LABEUVRIERE. Amb No 2. Journey to PHILOSOPHE.	
VAUDRICOURT			No 2 SECTION, Amb No 9. Journey to MAZINGARBE. Amb No 12 Journey to MAZINGARBE, Amb No 14 Journey to LABEUVRIERE,	

Army Form C. 2118

WAR DIARY
or
INTELLIGENCE SUMMARY
(Erase heading not required.)

15th Fd. Dn. N.L. A. Ambulance. Lower Forwards to End of Week

Place	Date	Hour	Summary of Events and Information	Remarks and references to Appendices
VAUDRICOURT	15/9/15	Wed.	No 2 SECTION (Cont'd). HESDIGNEUL & general duty. No 3 SECTION Collecting & Evacuating. Amb No 15, 29 a.b.; Amb No 18, 40 a.b.; Amb No 20, 10 a.b.; Amb No 21, 10 a.b.	B.W. etc. Lt/R.A.M.C.
HESDIGNEUL	16/9/15	Thurs.	WORKSHOP. Notably to 16 (No 3 sec'n) Repairing Panhard Pipe "Vidan" Brewy of 32 Sanitary Sec'n (?) Repairing Stretcher Chocks. One had car friendly in. Adjusting pressure valve. Carried cony men up the line. Divisional Staff Officers visited to Bn Ld at ROUAI. NO 1. SECTION. at Amb No 3. Journey to MAZINGARBE & GOSNAY; Amb No 4. Journey to BETHUNE & ST. OMER & Amb No 6 Journey to HESDIGNEUL & MOEUX-LES-MINES.	"
LABEUVRIERE				
NOEUX-LES-MINES			Amb No 1 & 7. Journey to PHILOSOPHE.	
VAUDRICOURT			No 2 SECTION Amb No 10 & 11. Journey to LILLERS. Amb No 12 & 13. Journey to VERQUIN, & LAPUGNOY.	"
NOEUX-LES-MINES			No 3 SECTION Collecting Evacuating. Amb No 15, 10 a.b.; Amb No 16, 28 a.b.; Amb No 17, 66 a.b.; Amb No 18, 19.3 a.b.; Amb No 20, 14 a.b.; Amb No 21, 38 a.b.	B.W. etc. Lt/R.A.M.C.
HESDIGNEUL	17/9/15	Fri.	WORKSHOP. To Columbuin (No 2 Sec) Spanning of Shaft gearing of Pump No 20 Ford Lt. The Ambulances broke out at the Valve of the getting new caps to strong first Africa tire. Various Long. (Bashful). Repairing right hub by fitting new rivets etc. Various Pumps' Sec'ny Sec'n) Repairing Crank. Soying costs. Varah to MOEUX-LES-MINES to inspect cars. Lieut BARKER and this in way to out Lycra Preenra. NO 1 SECTION Amb No 30 & 5. Journey to MOEUX-LES-MINES. Amb No 6. Journey to HESDIGNEUL.	"
LABEUVRIERE				

2353. Wt. W2544/1454. 700,000. 5/15. D.D.&L. A.D.S.S. Forms/C. 2118.

WAR DIARY
INTELLIGENCE SUMMARY

(Erase heading not required.) 15th Div. of Aux. Cols. A.S.C. M.J.

Army Form C. 2118

Place	Date	Hour	Summary of Events and Information	Remarks and references to Appendices
NOEUX-LES-MINES	17/9/15	Fri.	No 1. SECTION. Cont. Amb. No. 15 Y. Journey to LABEUVRIERE	On Field
VAUDRICOURT			No 2 SECTION. Amb. Nos. 8, 10, 11, 9, 12. Two journeys 9 No. 9. One journey to NOEUX-LES-MINES. Amb. No. 9. Journey to PHILOSOPHE. Amb. No. 10. Journey to Workshop & HESDIGNEUL. Amb. No. 11. Journey to LARUSNOK Amb. No. 14 Journey to BETHUNE. Amb. No. 13. Two journeys to LILLERS. Amb. No. 13. Two journeys to LARUSNOK Amb. No. 14 Journey to MAZINGARBE, district.	"
NOEUX-LES-MINES			No. 3 SECTION. Collecting & Evacuating. Amb. No. 15, 30 mls; Amb. No. 18, 10 mls; Amb. No. 19, 32 mls; Amb. No. 2, 0, 16 mls; Amb. No. 21, 74 mls. B.Butta Lt. A.S.C.	"
HESDIGNEUL	18/9/15	Sat.	WORKSHOP. Sunbeam No 10. C No 2 Section Leaking elongator box, easy solute rod plunger, & replacing gear box. Morris Lorry leaking tilting wind screen. Joined to AIRE to report to D.D. of S&T in morning. Staff Sgt. CUTLER gave driving instruction to 2nd Driver on Sunbeam section Lorry.	
LABEUVRIERE			No 1 SECTION. Amb. Nos. 3, & 6. Journey to HESDIGNEUL. No. 3. returning via NOEUX-LES-MINES. Amb. No. 3. Journey to LOZINGHEM. Amb. No. 5. Journey to LILLERS. Amb. No. 1. Two journeys to LABEUVRIERE.	
NOEUX-LES-MINES			No 2 SECTION. Amb. No. 9. Journey to LABEUVRIERE. Amb. No. 10. Journey to PHILOSOPHE. Amb. No. 13. Journey to HESDIGNEUL. Journey to NOEUX-LES-MINES 9 District & ST. VENANT.	
VAUDRICOURT				
NOEUX-LES-MINES			No 3 SECTION. Collecting & Evacuating. Amb. No. 15, 18 mls; Amb. No. 20, 10 mls (Bendechroean G) Amb. No. 21, 40 mls. B.Butta Lt. A.S.C.	

Army Form C. 2118

WAR DIARY
or
INTELLIGENCE SUMMARY.

(Erase heading not required.)

Instructions regarding War Diaries and Intelligence Summaries are contained in F.S. Regs., Part II. and the Staff Manual respectively. Title pages will be prepared in manuscript.

Place	Date	Hour	Summary of Events and Information	Remarks and references to Appendices
HESDIGNEUL	19/9/15	Sun	WORKSHOP. Forging fittings for stretcher.	Detail List
LABEUVRIERE			No 1 SECTION. Amb. Nos 4 & 6. Journeys to HESDIGNEUL. Amb. No 6 Journey to NOEUX-LES-MINES.	"
NOEUX-LES-MINES			Amb No 7. Journey to LABEUVRIERE, & MAZINGARBE.	
VAUDRICOURT			No 2 SECTION. Amb. No 8. Journey to MAZINGARBE, Amb No 10.11 Journey to Workshops at HESDIGNEUL. Amb No 12. Journey to PHILOSOPHE.	
NOEUX-LES-MINES			No 3 SECTION. Military Funeral; Amb No 15. 10 miles; Amb No 18, 2 miles; Amb No 20, 4 miles; Amb No 21. 20 m.s. Both M.T.A.C.
HESDIGNEUL	20/9/15	Mon	WORKSHOP. No Linehan. Checking up inspection, relaying instruction who No 11 Sun beam (No 28, sha.), taking down Radiator tank, clearing out scale in, re-soldering, repairing, A.D.M.S. hackney strutford, Ford sudden Vulcanising fpt. Moyel (Moidel) Repairing carrier. W(cycle No2 ea) Repairing & 2nd rear light cable.	
NOEUX-LES-MINES			No 1 SECTION. Amb No 3. Journey to LILLERS. Amb No 4. Journey to MAZINGARBE. Amb No 5. Journey to NOEUX-LES-MINES. Amb No 6 Journey to HESDIGNEUL. Amb. No 2. Own journey to MAZINGARBE & two to NOEUX-LES-MINES for Instruction.	
LABEUVRIERE			Amb No 1. Journey to MAZINGARBE & PHILOSOPHE. Amb No 2. Journey to MAZINGARBE & LABEUVRIERE	
VAUDRICOURT			No 2 SECTION. Amb No 8 Journey to Workshop Great. Amb No 9. Journey to PHILOSOPHE. Amb No 10 Journey to LILLERS. Amb No 11. Journey to HESDIGNEUL. & Workshops. Amb No 12. Workshops & LILLERS. Amb No 13, LA PHILOSOPHE & LOZINGHEN. Amb No 14 Journey to Amb No 14. Bucc to LA BEUVRIERE, twice to MAZINGARBE.	
NOEUX-LES-MINES			No 3. SECTION.	

WAR DIARY or INTELLIGENCE SUMMARY

Army Form C. 2118

15th Div. F. Amb.

Place	Date	Hour	Summary of Events and Information	Remarks and references to Appendices
HESDIGNEUL	2/9/15		WORKSHOP No 12. Sunbeam (No 2 Sect) Rebrazing inner tube. Steie bar, Straightened spick, Sunbeam car. looking over & fitted rear & considered same. A.D.M.S. Making shelter fittings. Voluntered to B.R.A.M.C. men of the 47th Div. Wallis & co. Divron.	
NOEUX-LES-MINES			No 1 SECTION. Amb. No. 1. Journey to MAZINGARBE. Amb No 7. Journey to HESDIGNEUL. Amb No 2. Journey to MAZINGARBE.	"
LABEUVRIERE			Amb. No. 6. Journey to HESDIGNEUL. Amb. Nos 3 & 5. Journey to NOEUX-LES-MINES. Amb. No. 5. Brought from LABEUVRIERE to NOEUX-LES-MINES.	"
VAUDRICOURT			No 2 SECTION. Ambs No. 8 & 11. Journey to PHILOSOPHE, & LOZINGHEM. Amb. No. 13. Journey to HESDIGNEUL to be used for evacuation purposes. Did one journey to PHILOSOPHE.	"
NOEUX-LES-MINES			No 3 SECTION Collecting evacuating. Amb No. 17. 6 m.b. Amb No. 19. 22 m.b. Amb No. 20. 5 m.b. Amb. 6. 21. 10 m.b. B. Sheller & A.A.C.	
HESDIGNEUL	28/9/15		WORKSHOP No 9 Sunbeam. (No 2 Sect) Repairing head lamp. Screen brings. Fitting generator. Sunbeam car. tubing & fitting new screen frame. Photo cycle (No 2 Sect) Repairing spring forks. A.D.M.S. turning shutter fittings. Levard to BETHUNE to purchase item. Staff Workshops Staff road to Bethuel & BRUAY.	"
NOEUX-LES-MINES			No. 1 SECTION. Amb. No. 7 Journey HESDIGNEUL Amb. No. 2. Journey to MAZINGARBE.	
MAZINGARBE			Amb No. 2. Journey to BETHUNE & NOEUX-LES-MINES.	
LABEUVRIERE			Amb. No. 4. Journey to CHOCQUES & LAPUGNOY.	
VAUDRICOURT			No 2 SECTION. Amb. No. 9. Journey to FOUQUIERES, PHILOSOPHE, & ? Amb. No. 10. Journey to FOUQUIERES & LOZINGHEM. Amb. No. 13. Two journeys to PHILOSOPHE. Amb. No. 14. Journey to MAZINGARBE.	"

WAR DIARY or INTELLIGENCE SUMMARY.

Army Form C. 2118

(Erase heading not required.)

15th Divl. T.A.S.C.

Place	Date	Hour	Summary of Events and Information	Remarks and references to Appendices
NOEUX-LES-MINES	22/9/15	Wed.	No 3. SECTION Collecting & Issuing rations. Amb No 1B, 5 mls. Amb No 20, 10 mls. Amb No 21, 8 mls.	B.Shels to Wksh. Detail in field
HESDIGNEUL	23/9/15	Thurs.	WORKSHOP. Motor cycle (No 3. Sect.). Repairing damage caused by accident. Ford (No 2. SECTION) fitting new spring.	"
			Ford lorry. Ford No 20. (No 3 Sect) Repairing mudguard. Sunbeam car. Making socket for screen.	
			SECTION No. 1.	
NOEUX-LES-MINES			Amb No 6, 7. Journey to HESDIGNEUL. Amb No. 2. Journey from MAZINGARBE to VERMELLES & return. Amb No 4.	"
LABEUVRIERE			Journey from LABEUVRIERE to MAZINGARBE & LOZINGHEM. Amb No 4. Journey from LABEUVRIERE to NOEUX-LES-MINES	"
			Amb No 2. Journey from the abattoir to NOEUX-LES-MINES.	
VAUDRICOURT			No. 2. SECTION (Amb No 8, 10, 11. Journey to PHILOSOPHE. No. 12, to PHILOSOPHE & LAPUGNOY. Amb No. 2 to	"
			LILLERS & ST. VENANT. Amb No 10. to LOZINGHEM. Amb No. 13. to DROUVIN, Amb No 14. to VERQUIN.	
NOEUX-LES-MINES			No. 3. SECTION. Collecting & Issuing rations. Amb No 16. 20 mls: Amb No. 19. 16 mls: Amb No. 6. 20, 28 mls.:	Shells to W.Shop
HESDIGNEUL	24/9/15	Frid.	WORKSHOP. No. 11. Sunbeam (No 2 Sect.) Repairing outlet tank & adjusting steering. Staff lorry. Fitting rail for	"
			carrying cars on top. Cab. bodyshop. Shaking tailb. Ford. I went to BETHUNE for shade (?) carrying glasses?	
			for repair. Tool loaned to 4th F.A. Ambulance at VAUDRICOURT	
MAZINGARBE			No. 1. SECTION Amb No 2. Three journeys to NOEUX-LES-MINES.	
NOEUX-LES-MINES			Amb No. 6. Journey to HESDIGNEUL. Amb No. 7. Journey to MAZINGARBE.	
VAUDRICOURT			No. 2. SECTION. Amb No. 8, 9, 10, 13. Journey to NOEUX-LES-MINES & PHILOSOPHE. Amb No. 12. to Workshop. Amb No 00, 11, 12, to	
			NOEUX-LES-MINES. Amb. No. 13. Journey to LABUGNOY. Amb. No. 14. Journey to NOEUX-LES-MINES.	

WAR DIARY
or
INTELLIGENCE SUMMARY.
(Erase heading not required.)

Army Form C. 2118

15th Div. 3/A.M.C. A.C.C. M.T.

Place	Date	Hour	Summary of Events and Information	Remarks and references to Appendices
NOEUX-LES-MINES	24/9/15	3rd.	No. 3 SECTION. Utterly unworkmanly. Amb. No. 15. Friday, And No. 18. 10 a.m. And No. 19. 20. And No. 21. 20. Distributed to H.Q. D. Field Ambs.	
HESDIGNEUL	25/9/15	Sat.	WORKSHOP. Starting. Jolly chubic full of hot dry lookshop day. Working fifty linklets for sub-schools. The big shaking lorries under lamp. Used 8 HRE in morning to April 6.20 p.m. 17. In afternoon parade with 10 high. CUTLER & NORTH.	"
			LES-MINES, VERMELLES & in port with lines to division, still busy at lorry station during attack.	
NOEUX-MINES	25/9/15		No.1 SECTION. Amb. No. 4, Journey to HESDIGNEUIL. Amb. No. 1-9 proceeded to PHILOSOPHE, "QUALITY" STREET & HAZINGARBE wounded 4, wounded to NOEUX-LES-MINES, VAUDRICOURT, & LA RUGNOY, started at 10.45 a.m. & continued till 2.10 a.m. on	"
			Sunday 26/9/15. The drivers working in relief.	
			No. 2 SECTION. All ambulances started clearing wounded from PHILOSOPHE & VAUDRICOURT & NOEUX-LES-MINES & LA PUGNOY & OZINGHEM. " R.W. Hick & R.A.M.C.	"
			at 9 a.m. 25/9/15 & continued till 9 a.m. 27/9/15.	
			No. 3 SECTION. All ambulances clearing wounded from "QUALITY" STREET, & PHILOSOPHE & NOEUX-LES-MINES R.W. Hick & R.A.M.C.	"
HESDIGNEUL	26/9/15	Sun.	WORKSHOP. Ford No. 21 Chas 3 Sab? Before midday, lining of brg (Middl A) Sunbeam No. 2 (16/Sub) R.H.Q. new plate. Belt near Crabi-Shine, Wolseley No. 17 (2nd Sub) Graylling 2 vans, 2 valve stems, & 4 spark plugs. Laurel & NOEUX-LES-MINES 9	"
			LILLERS in morning & then about Rebel & HQ in evening used "QUALITY" STREET will HARRIER lorry & to her first church Helenda Kavrin, lorry got filled from WAR REQUESTS in morning, PATOUR 6 Km out & LILLERS at night in medical store.	
			No.1 SECTION. Same as previous day.	
			No.2 SECTION. Same as previous day.	
			No.3 SECTION. Same as previous day. Ambulances clearing wounded from LOOS.	

B. Newton VAD R.A.M.C.

Army Form C. 21

WAR DIARY
or
INTELLIGENCE SUMMARY.

(Erase heading not required.) 13th Div. 1/2 H. Ambulance to Hospital H.R.C.M.Y

Instructions regarding War Diaries and Intelligence Summaries are contained in F. S. Regs. Part II. and the Staff Manual respectively. Title pages will be prepared in manuscript.

Place	Date	Hour	Summary of Events and Information	Remarks and references to Appendices
HESDIGNEUL.	27/9/15	Mon.	WORKSHOP. Ford No 13 (No 2 Sec), fitting Westinghouse Belt. Ford No. 20. (No 3. Sec). Taking down back axle, fitting new propeller shaft casing. Adjusting coils, turning up & testing car. 2nd and of HOMER obtained new Ford axle from 35th C.V.S.C. M.T. Ryan Lieut. Harrier Lorry Knight 600 gals of petrol from WIRDRECQUES.	
NOEUX-LES-MINES.			No 1 SECTION. All ambulances evacuating wounded from PHILOSOPHE, "QUALITY" STREET & LOOS, also to the abattoir at MAZINGARBE & then from MAZINGARBE to NOEUX-LES-MINES. Also No. S. Sectioning 15 MAZINGARBE.	
VAUDRICOURT.			No 2 SECTION All ambulances evacuating from LILLERS to NERVILLE, & from VAUDRICOURT to LILLERS, LOZINGHEM	
NOEUX-LES-MINES			No 3 SECTION All Ambulances Collecting from LOOS, PHILOSOPHE, & VERMELLES. B.E. Hutton Lt. K. A.C.	
HESDIGNEUL.	28/9/15.	Tues.	WORKSHOP. Ford No 13 (No 2 Sec) Repairing hand tyre & tuning up engine. Ford No 21. Fitting two new tyres & winning tappet. Sliding bracket for rear lamp. Ford to MAZINGARBE & injured ambulance. Harrier Lorry two journeys to NOEUX-LES-MINES.	
NOEUX-LES-MINES			No 1 SECTION All ambulances evacuating from hospital station, then from NOEUX-LES-MINES to LILLERS, & on L.N.Y. Journey to LILLERS.	
			HESDIGNEUL. Ambces Nos 1, 3, 4, 5 from evacuating connected to LABOURSE. Also No. 2. Journey to PHILOSOPHE.	
VAUDRICOURT.			No 2. SECTION. No Detail.	
			No. 3 SECTION. All ambulances evacuating. B.E. Hutton Lt. V.A.C.	
HESDIGNEUL.	29/9/15	Wed.	WORKSHOP Ford No. 1 (No 1 Sec) Aufradig clutch, front wheel covers, tuning up engine, testing car. Harrier Lorry, impossible to start for new spring. A.D.M.S. Refilling officer dark truck. Bicycle (No 1 Sec) Repairing priof tubes, carrier, retail etc. Loved BETHUNE for gums to DROUIN & LABUISSIERE.	

B.E. Hutton Lt. V.A.C.

2353   Wt. W2544/1454   700,000   5/15   D. D. & L.   A.D.S.S. Forms/C. 2118.

Army Form C. 2118

WAR DIARY
or
INTELLIGENCE SUMMARY.

(Erase heading not required.) 15th Div Field Ambulance / RAMC

Place	Date	Hour	Summary of Events and Information	Remarks and references to Appendices
NOEUX-LES-MINES	29/9/15 Wed.		No. 1 SECTION. Amb. No. 6 Journey to MAXINGARBE. Ambulances moved from NOEUX-LES-MINES to meet train at HESDIGNEUL.	Duty field
VAUDRICOURT			No. 2 SECTION. Amb. No. 8. Journey to HALLICOURT. Amb. No. 14 Journey to PHILOSOPHE.	"
NOEUX-LES-MINES			No. 3 SECTION. Collecting wounded city. Ambs. 18, 10 mls. Amb. No. 12, 12 mls. Amb. 1 No. 20, 20 mls.	B.E.Lutton Lt Col RAMC?
HESDIGNEUL	30/9/15 Thurs.		WORKSHOP. Sanitar No. 8 (No. 2 Sect.) Making door frames and straightening axle & repairing radiator & mudguard Ford No. 21. (No. 3 Sect.) Adjusting steering of Ford. studs, spanning bodywork, tuning up engine etc etc. Workshops moved from HESDIGNEUL to LABUISSIERE.	"
HESDIGNEUL			No. 1 SECTION. Amb. No. 1. Journey to NOEUX-LES-MINES. Amb. No. 6. Journey to LAPUGNOY. Amb. No. 3. Journey to LABUISSIERE. No. 1 Section moved from HESDIGNEUL to LABUISSIERE.	"
VAUDRICOURT			No. 2 SECTION. Amb. No. 8 to Lockhilly. Amb. No. 10. Journey to LILLERS to district. Amb. No. 11, 13 Journey to HALLICOURT. Amb. No. 12. Journey to HOUCHIN. Amb. No. 14. General duty.	"
NOEUX-LES-MINES			No. 3. SECTION. Medical Stores Amb. No. 15, 14 mls. Amb. No. 16, 17 & 18. 8 mls. each. Amb. No. 20 & 21. 8 mls. each. Amb. No. 17, 10 mls. evacuating. No. 3. Section moved from NOEUX-LES-MINES to HALLICOURT.	" B.E.Lutton Lt Col RAMC.

121/7517

15th/K/15 warrin

15th Divl. F.a.w.v.
roe 4
Oct 15

Orig 3

WAR DIARY or INTELLIGENCE SUMMARY

Army Form C. 2118

October 1915 15th Div'l Fd M[...] Workshop [...] A.C.M.T.

Place	Date	Hour	Summary of Events and Information	Remarks and references to Appendices
LABUISSIERE	1/10/15		**WORKSHOP** Ford No.6. (No.1 Sec'n) Having fitting Engine & Repairing generator. B/cycle (No.1 Sec'n) making & fitting brake adjuster. Turning new fork pins. B/cycle (No.2 Sec'n) Repairing cacb [carb?] & fitting & tightening chain. Motorcycle No.17. (No.3 Sec'n) Re-straightening engine & fitting new bracket, repairing carrier & forks. Ford No.13 (No.2 sec'n) fitting new spring clip. Sunbeam No.1. fitting new crank foring bolts & repairing horn. Sunbeam No.3. Repairing cab brake ratchet. Sunbeam No.4. (No.1 Sec'n) Straightening handle & turning & fitting new rods for rear wheel. Sunbeam No.5 (No.1 Sec'n) Adjusting brakes & fitting bolts in wing stay. Pte Cousins drove Sunbeam car 62 mls. for A.D.M.S. staff.	Enlisted
			No.1 SECTION Amb No.2 Journey to VAUDRICOURT & LILLERS. Amb No.3. Journey to NOEUX-LES-MINES. Amb No.4. Journey to HESDIGNEUL.	B. Enfield
LAPUGNOY			Amb. No.6 Journey to BETHUNE. Amb No.1. Journey to [illegible]	
VAUDRICOURT			**No.2 SECTION** Amb No.3 Journey to GOSSNAY. Amb. No.11 Journey to HALLICOURT. Amb. No.13. Journey to LA BOURSE. Amb. No.14. Journey to MAXINGARBE district.	
NOEUX-LES-MINES			**No.3 SECTION** Collecting & Evacuating. Amb No.15. 17 mls; Amb No.16. 14 mls; Amb No.17. 4 mls; Amb. No.18. 24 mls; Amb No.20. 24 mls; Amb. No.21. 10 mls;	B.E. [illegible]
LABUISSIERE	2/10/15		**WORKSHOP** Sunbeam No.5. fitting new rear spring centre pin. (No.1 Sec'n) Sunbeam No.2. (No.1 Sec'n) fitting new spring centre pin & adjusting brakes. W. B'cley (No.12) (No.3 Sec'n) Repairing body covering, truing & fitting new fork & fitting new spring fork pins. (Sec'n) Turning new spring fork pins. I went to MPRE ST. OMER with A.D.M.S.	"

Army Form C. 2118

WAR DIARY
or
INTELLIGENCE SUMMARY.

(Erase heading not required.) (5th Div. Field Amb. Workshop Med Adv. C. Dep.)

Instructions regarding War Diaries and Intelligence Summaries are contained in F.S. Regs., Part II. and the Staff Manual respectively. Title pages will be prepared in manuscript.

Place	Date	Hour	Summary of Events and Information	Remarks and references to Appendices
LABUISSIERE	2/10/15	Sat.	No 1 SECTION. (contd) Amb. No. 6. Journey to NOEUX-LES-MINES. Amb. No. 7. General Duty.	Distributed
			No 2. SECTION. Amb. Nos. 8 & 12, Journey to NOEUX-LES-MINES district. Amb. No. 9. Journey to HAZEBROUCK district. Amb. No. 10.	"
			Journey to LAPUGNOY. Amb. No. 11. to "GORE" BRIDGE. Amb. No. 13. to ST. VENANT. No. 14. to LABOURSE.	
NOEUX-LES-MINES			No 3 SECTION Collecting wounded. Amb. No. 15. 7 nbc; Amb. No. 16. 12 nbc. Amb. No. 17. 7 nbc (3 to Lavre batpx)	
			Amb. No. 18. 7 nbc (2 to No. batpx). Amb. No. 19. 12 nbc; Amb. No. 20. 14 nbc; Amb. No. 21. 20 nbc.	
			B. Bulten Lt. A.S.C.	
LABUISSIERE	3/10/15	Sunday	WORKSHOP. Motor cycle (No. 1 Sec.). Leaving fitting & being forked sackles. Lorry being held until moved to LAPUGNOY.	
LABUISSIERE			No 1 SECTION. Amb. No. 7. Journey to HESDIGNEUL. Amb. No. 6. Journey to BROUVAIN. Amb. No. 3 to join journey to LAPUGNOY. One journey to LILLERS.	
			Amb. M. et. Journey to ALLOUAGNE. No. 1 Sec. moved to ALLOUAGNE. Amb. No. 5 Journey to LILLERS.	
			No. 2. SECTION. Amb. Nos. 8, 9, 10. Journey to HALLICOURT. Amb. No. 10. Journey to LABOURSE. Amb. No. 11 & 12. Journey to NOEUX-LES-MINES.	
			Amb. No. 13 Journey to HESDIGNEUL.	
LILLERS			No. 3 SECTION. Moved from NOEUX-LES-MINES to LILLERS. Amb. No. 15. 10 nbc; Amb. No. 16. 26 nbc; Amb. No. 17. 10 nbc; Amb. No. 18.	
			14 nbc; Amb. No. 19. 16 nbc; Amb. No. 20. 20 nbc; Amb. No. 21. 36 nbc.	
			B. Bulten Lt. A.S.C.	
LAPUGNOY	4/10/15		WORKSHOP. Magneto (No. 1 Sec.) Fitting tyres & shackles to Ford Lorries. Ford No. 21 (No. 3 sec.) straightening air port. Walnuts Nos. 17 (No. 3 sec) &	
			Setting flat axle arm & truing-up front wheels. Small tools Harris lorry & Ford 6/cycles from the 5th Div. Supply Column.	

WAR DIARY or INTELLIGENCE SUMMARY

Army Form C. 2118

Place	Date	Hour	Summary of Events and Information	Remarks and references to Appendices
ALLOUAGNE	4/10/15	Mor.	(Contd) No.1 SECTION. Amb. No.1. to AIRE. Amb. No.4. to LABEUVRIERE. Amb. No.5.7. Local journeys by Amb. No. 3 & 6. Journeys 26.61 mls.	In field
			LILLERS. Amb. No.2. to LOZINGHEM.	
VAUDRICOURT			No 2 SECTION. Amb. No.8. to ALLOUAGNE. Amb. No.10. to LILLERS. Various Amb. No.14. to BETHUNE.	
LILLERS.			No 3 SECTION. Amb. Nos. 15, 16, 18, & 20. Road 20 mls for medical Stores. Amb. Nos. 17 & 21 to Lordships, &c &c light	
			14 mls each. Amb. No. 19. Medical Stores & cements, 32 mls	
				B. Lieut. N.H.A.C.
LAPUGNOY	5/10/15	Lno.	WORKSHOP. Wolseley No. 19. Straightening tie rod & lining up steels, & Repairing car no body. Wolseley 16.	
			Lifting centre pin on front spring. Fitting wooden batten on side of body. Wyrd (M. Lee.) Repairing saddle	
			spring, adjusting steering head. Sunbeam car. Making fittings for rear L. spring. Sterris Lorry. Taking down	
			bracket, & boring slides spring bracket.	
ALLOUAGNE.			No 1 SECTION. Amb. No. 1. Journeys to Lookshop for repairs, & to LILLERS. Amb. No. 4. In Journey. Amb. No. 7. Two Journeys to LILLERS.	
			Amb. No. 5. Journey to CHOQUES. Amb. No. 6. Journey to LABEUVRIETE & LAPUGNOY.	
VAUDRICOURT.			No 2 SECTION. Staff in moved from VAUDRICOURT to MARLES-LES-MINES. Amb. No. 9. Journey to LILLERS. Amb. No. 13	
			Journey to LAPUGNOY. Amb. No. 8. Local took Amb. Nos. 10, 11 & 12 Journeys from ALLOUAGNE now to MARLES-LES-MINES.	
LILLERS.			No 3 SECTION. Orderly Evacuating medical Stores. Amb. No. 15. & his. Amb. No. 16. & to 6th Lookshop for repairs. Amb. No. 17.	
			10 mls; Amb. No.19. 14 mls; (to Workshops) Amb. No. 20. 32 mls; Amb. No. 21. 12 mls.	
				B. Lieut. N.H.A.C.

WAR DIARY or INTELLIGENCE SUMMARY.

Army Form C. 2118.

(Erase heading not required.)

Place	Date	Hour	Summary of Events and Information	Remarks and references to Appendices
LAPUGNOY	6/10/15	Wed.	WORKSHOP No 16 Lorries lay. (No 3 Sec) hacking filling woods & rebuilding bodies, Harris Lorry Lining up P.H. B.E.F.V.Wd. new pins & filling of sliding bracket. Crossen Car refitting new axle & crown. Winchester 4.5 T.H. not delivered.	
MARLES-LES-MINES			P.H. ambulance at LILLERS.	
ALLOUAGNE			No 1 SECTION Ambe Nos 1, 2, & 6 Journey to LOZINGHEM. Ambe No 2 Journey to CHOCQUES, LOZINGHEM & LILLERS. Ambe No 4 Journey to CHOCQUES & RETHUNE. Ambe No 5 Journey to LAPUGNOY LILLERS. Ambe No 9 Journey to LAPUGNOY. Ambe No 7 Journey to LILLERS & ARQUES.	
MARLES-MINES			No 2 SECTION Ambe No 3, 10, & 12 Journey to LILLERS. Ambe No 11 Journey to LILLERS & civilied.	
			No 3 SECTION Ambe No 15, Lorabolope. Bath. Ambe No 17, 26 wk (Whaley Warner), Ambe No 18 2 wk. Ambe No 20, 10 wk (overall). Amb No 21, 12 wk (husk ed Clors)	B.Ruth V.H.K.C.
LAPUGNOY	7/10/15	Thurs.	WORKSHOP Harris Lorry fitting packing piece, pins & body & rear shaft. Whaley No 5 (No 3 Sec.) fitting wood batons on body. Crossen No 11 (No 2 Sec.) lining up & taking engine.	
ALLOUAGNE			No 1 SECTION Ambe No 1 & 7 Journey to LILLERS. Ambe No 6 Journey to ARQUES & LAPUGNOY. Ambe No 8 Journey to BRUAY. Ambe No 9 Journey to LOZINGHEM.	
MARLES-MINES			No 2 SECTION Ambe No 8 & 12 of to CHOCQUES. Ambe No 9 Journey to BETHUNE. Ambe No 11 & Lor billposter No 13 Sore Journey to LILLERS. Ambe No 14. Journey to Lorabolope & LILLERS & Lodaich. Sergt. FRANKLIN (No 2 Sec) Road Kingland on 3 days leave.	
			No 3 SECTION Ambe No 15, 11 wk. Ambe No 17, 6 wk. Ambe No 19, 4 wk. Ambe No 20, 26 wk. Ambe No 21, 17 wk.	B.R.W. H.R.K.C.

Army Form C. 2118

WAR DIARY
or
INTELLIGENCE SUMMARY

(Erase heading not required.) 15th Div'l ? ? ? ? A.S.C. ?

Place	Date	Hour	Summary of Events and Information	Remarks and references to Appendices
LAPUGNOY	8/10/15	Fri.	WORKSHOP Sunbeam No.11 (No 2 Sub) Lining of wheels, fitting new brake officer and spring clips. Motor cycle (No 2 Sec.) lighting chair rebuilt. Sunbeam Car fitted petrol can carrier. Motor cycle (No 2 sec.) staying for repairs for leaving Saturday ? a.m. I left for England on 6 days leave as also did Sergt. BARKER.	Detail filed
			No. 1 SECTION. Ambs. No.s 1,2,6,7. Journey to LAPUGNOY. Amb. No. 4 Journey to LOZINGHEM. Amb. No. 6 Local work & Journey to	"
ALLOUAGNE			CHOCQUES. Amb. No. 3 Journey to ARQUES.	"
MARIES-LES-MINES			No 2 SECTION. Work. No.11 Journey to Workshops. Amb No.13 Journey to LILLERS.	"
LILLERS.			No 3 SECTION. Collecting & evacuating. Amb. No.16. ? Amb. No.15. Amb. No.19. 14 m.b. Amb No.10. 29 m.b. ? Amb. No.21. 14 m.b.	"
				B Ed ??? Lt. H.A.C.
LAPUGNOY.	9/10/15	Sat.	WORKSHOP. Harris Lorry taking down of petrol wheels & bearers relining for brakes. Wolsley No.19 (No 3 Sec.) Repairs to body refitting fire extinguisher. Harris Lorry Loryy silluij ting tracks. Lee CAFRANCE sent to Supply Column to see about requisition of supplies.	"
			No 1 SECTION. Amb. No. 7 Journey to LILLERS. Ambs. Nos. 5,6,9. Journeys to LAPUGNOY. Amb No.6 Journey to ARQUES. Amb. No. 5.	"
ALLOUAGNE.			Journey to LOZINGHEM. Amb. No. 4. Journey to BRUAY.	"
MARIES-LES-MINES			No 2 SECTION. Amb. No.4. Journey to LILLERS & CHOCQUES.	"
LILLERS.			No 3 SECTION. Collecting & evacuating. Amb. No.16. 28 m.b.s. (Sitroen & horse). Amb. No.17. 7 m.b.; Amb. No. 20. 14 m.b.; Amb. No. 21. 16 m.b.s.	"
				B Ed ??? Lt.H.A.C.

WAR DIARY or INTELLIGENCE SUMMARY

Army Form C. 2118

Place	Date	Hour	Summary of Events and Information	Remarks and references to Appendices
LAPUGNOY	10/10/15	Sun	WORKSHOP. Relegate (No 3 Sect). Fitter aussisting to Forbes Gleaner Lorry. Lamplighter Cab & cook refreshments. Intelligible. A Tilley Lorry. Relegate (No 2 Sect) Various sundry jobs, firewood. Lieut-Col PRINCE went to Supply Column to have Indicator signed by C/M. SMITH. A.D.M.S. Employed car.	"
ALLOUAGNE			No. 1 SECTION. Ambs. Nos. 2, 4, 7. Journeys to LILLERS. Ambs Nos. 4, 6 Journeys to LAPUGNOY. Amb. No. 6, Journey to CHOCQUES. Amb. No. 5. Journey to 139 C.A.S.C.	"
MARLES-LES-MINES			No. 2 SECTION. Amb. No. 13. Journey to KNEPPER, district (9 ords). Amb. No. 14. Two Journeys to LILLERS.	"
			No. 3 SECTION. Collecting & evacuating, Amb. No. 18. 6 miles, Amb. No. 20.19 mls, Amb. No. 21, 24 mls. B9 Lutter H.A.C.	"
LAPUGNOY	11/10/15	Mon	WORKSHOP. Sundries No. 2. (No 1 Sect) Allegro new centre bolt, tour spring, Relegate (No 2 Sect) Various jobs, firebars inordinate.	"
			Staff workshop staff went to Baths at BRUAY. A.D.M.S. used Workshop Car.	
ALLOUAGNE			No. 1 SECTION. Amb. No. 2. Two journeys & Amb. Nos. 3, 4, 5 & 6 one journey each to LAPUGNOY. Amb. No. 4 Journey to LILLERS & APUGNOY.	"
			Return to ARQUES.	
MARLES-LES-MINES			No. 2 SECTION. Amb. No. 10. Journey to "QUALITY STREET" & district. Amb. No. 12 Journey to LAPUGNOY. Amb. No. 13. Journey to COLONNE.	
			Amb. No. 14. Journey to ARQUES.	
			No. 3 SECTION. Amb. No. 15. 28 mls. (Officers to HAZEBROUCK). Amb. No. 19, 34 mls. (Officers to ST OMER) Amb. No. 21. 34 mls. Collecting and evacuating)	
			B9 Lutter H.A.C.	

WAR DIARY or INTELLIGENCE SUMMARY.

Army Form C. 2118

(Erase heading not required.) 15th Div: Tr: Fld: Ambulances: work of the 1st A.I.C.M.T.

Place	Date	Hour	Summary of Events and Information	Remarks and references to Appendices
LAPUGNOY.	12/10/15		WORKSHOP. Various Lorry Repairs to Superstructure. Lu/Cpl. Hobson the 2 Girls Hardening tyres took him that No. 20 fitting new type. Detached.	
ALLOUAGNE			Mtr. A.D.M.S. used out on Sunbeam Car.	
to			No.1 SECTION. Amb.No.1 Journey to LILLERS + BETHUNE. Amb.No.4 Journey via HOUCHAIN, BETHUNE, HOUCHAIN.	"
HALLICOURT.			HALLICOURT, & HOUCHAIN. Amb No. 5 Journey to LAPUGNOY. Amb Nos. 1,2,3. Journey via LOZINGHEM, LAPUGNOY & LILLERS. Amb No.7 Journey to	
			ARQUES. All ambulances moved from ALLOUAGNE to HALLICOURT.	
MARLES-LES-MINES.			No.2 SECTION. Amb.No.13. Two Journeys to LAPUGNOY.	"
LILLERS. &			No.3 SECTION. All ambulances moved from LILLERS to LOZINGHEM.	"
LOZINGHEM.			20. 36nls. Amb.No. 21. 24nls.	
LAPUGNOY.	13/10/15	W.D.	WORKSHOP. Various Lorry fitting + workshop fires under repairs. Effect of Fuel. No. 7 Motorcycle (Nobles) came in to workshop	B.Blth. Lt.F.A.C.
			with cracked differential case. Lu.Cpl. PRINCE does not drive with skill due to the slippy Roads for experience.	
HALLICOURT.			No.1 SECTION. Amb.No.4+6. Journeys to LAPUGNOY. Amb. Nos. 1,5+7. Journeys to LILLERS. Amb.No.6 Journey to NOEUX-LES-MINES.	"
MARLES-LES-MINES			No.2. SECTION. Amb. No. 14 Journey to LILLERS + District (General Work).	"
LOZINGHEM			No.3. SECTION. Chiefly Laundry. Amb.No.18. 12nls. Amb.No.20. 22nls. Amb.No. 21. 12nls.	B.Blth. Lt.F.A.C.
LAPUGNOY.	14/10/15	Thurs	WORKSHOP. Cleaning up Workshop. Store Lorry + Camp. Half Lorries of Staff went to Roll at TROUAY.	
HALLICOURT.			No.1 SECTION. Amb.No. 7. Lorry Journey via No. 6. One Journey to Refilly Point. Amb. No.1. Journey to NOEUX-LES-MINES. Amb. No. 7.	"
			Journey via LAPUGNOY, HOUCHAIN, + LOZINGHEM.	

Army Form C. 2118

WAR DIARY
or
INTELLIGENCE SUMMARY.
(Erase heading not required.) 15th Div Lift Mobile workshop Unit 2 M T

Instructions regarding War Diaries and Intelligence Summaries are contained in F. S. Regs., Part II. and the Staff Manual respectively. Title pages will be prepared in manuscript.

Place	Date	Hour	Summary of Events and Information	Remarks and references to Appendices
MARLES-LES-MINES	14/10/15	noon	(1) No 2 SECTION Ambulance not used. SERGT. FRANKLIN returned from leave.	Detail B/d.
LOZINGHEM to LABEUVRIERE			No. 3. SECTION All Ambulances except No. 19 (at workshop) moved station from LOZINGHEM to LABEUVRIERE. Ambs. Nos. 18, 20, 32 also dispatched (cook).	R.S. Allen R.F.M.C.
LAPUGNOY.	15/10/15	Sid.	WORKSHOP. Cleaning & packing up ready for moving.	"
HALLICOURT			No. 1. SECTION. Amb. No. 7. Journey to Refilling Point. Amb. No. 2. Long Journeys to NOEUX-LES-MINES.	"
MARLES-LES-MINES to HOUCHAIN			No. 2. SECTION. All ambulances moved to HOUCHAIN. Amb. Nos. 9, 10, 13, 14 during the journey. Amb. No. 14. General duty.	"
LABEUVRIERE.			No. 3. SECTION. Amb. No. 20, 21, 32 nls (for Interconnection) Amb. No. 21, 32 nls (Officer hanford)	B.L. Allen R.F.M.C
LAPUGNOY & NOEUX-LES-MINES	16/10/15	Sat.	WORKSHOP. Moved Camp from LAPUGNOY to NOEUX-LES-MINES. Included four cars, various longstored No. 9 Workshops and lorries.	"
NOEUX-LES-MINES			No 1 SECTION. All Ambulances moved from HALLICOURT to NOEUX-LES-MINES. Amb No. 2. Journey to Refg Refilling Point. Amb. No. 6. Journey to LILLERS. Amb. No. 7. Journey to HALLICOURT.	"
HOUCHIN.			No. 2. SECTION. Amb. No. 14. Journey from HOUCHAIN to ST. VENANT.	
HALLICOURT.			No 3. SECTION. Station moved from LABEUVRIERE to HALLICOURT. Amb. No. 18. Amb. No. 16, 32 nls, ammo passengers duty. Amb. No. 20, 21. 32 nls. Duty to Hallicourt Eneavohing	" B.L. Allen R.F.M.C.
NOEUX-LES-MINES.	17/10/15	Sun.	WORKSHOP. Sunbeam Car. Running Rear wheels, & clearing brake shoes drums. Lorry No. 19. Running body & steering wheel rear axle.	
			No. 1 SECTION. Amb. No. 7. Journey to NOEUX-PETIT-SANS HALLICOURT & detail general duty. Amb. No. 2. Workshop. Amb. No. 6. Journey to LABEUVRIERE.	"
NOEUX-LES-MINES.			No. 2. SECTION. Amb. No. 8. Journey to NOEUX-LES-MINES & district. Amb. No. 14. Two Journeys to LABUISSIERE, rear to NOEUX-LES-MINES.	

WAR DIARY or INTELLIGENCE SUMMARY

Army Form C. 2118

(Erase heading not required.) 15th Dist ADS ?th MD Mech Transport ASC Unit ADS MT

Place	Date	Hour	Summary of Events and Information	Remarks and references to Appendices
HALLICOURT.	17/10/15	Sun.	No.3. SECTION. Amb. No. 15. 12 wds. (Officers transport). Amb. No. 18. 20 wds. (Medical stores). Amb. No. 20. 20 wds. (Clearing). Amb. No. 21. 20 wds. (Clearing). Amb No. 21. District Field 28 wds. (Clearing & Forwarding).	B.E. Walton Lt. R.A.M.C.
NOEUX-LES-MINES.	18/10/15	h.a.	WORKSHOP. Wolsely No.19 & No.3. Set) Dismantling differential. Ford No.14 (No.2 Set) Repairing generator. Stu. Essex Repairing mudguard. Lassier. Turning sleeve for spring pin. Buick No.10 (No.2 Set) Renewing rear wheels & easy brakes. Fitting up 10 field cars carriers for ambulance. Ford No.20. Repairing generator. During the day 1 Buick & 5 R.A.M.C. men of the 46 Cy. Field Ambulance as drivers followers & turners 3 passed. Inspected Ambulances of 46th & 47th Field Ambulances.	"
NOEUX-LES-MINES.			No.1. SECTION. Amb. No. 7. Journeys to HALLICOURT, to workshops, to BETHUNE, ARQUES. Amb. No.6. Journeys to NOEUX - PETIT-SANS, to PHILOSOPHE, & to HALLICOURT. Amb. No. 1 & 5. Journeys to LILLERS.	"
HOUCHAIN.			No.2. SECTION. Amb. No. 11. 2 workshops for repairs to lorries. R.A.M.C. men as drivers.	"
HALLICOURT.			No.3. SECTION. Amb. No.12. 12 wds. (Clearing). Amb. No.20, 12 wds. (M.T. Stores). Amb. No. 21. 6 wds. (Medical Stores).	B.E. Walton Lt. R.A.M.C.
NOEUX-LES-MINES.	19/10/15.	Tues.	WORKSHOP. No.17 Wolsely (No.3 Set) Removing cylinder, removing carbon deposit & grinding in valves. Fitting to Study No. 17. (No.3 Set) Straightening front ? frame windows. Wolsely (No.1Set) Fitting new carrier. Ford No. 6. (No. 1 Set) Repairing system No. 5. making front car carrier	"
HALLICOURT.			No.1. SECTION. Amb. No.1. 2 journeys to HALLICOURT. Amb. No.6. Journey to NOEUX-PETIT-SA VS. Amb. No. 2. Journey to BETHUNE. (General duty) Amb. No.3. Journey to ARQUES.	"
NOEUX-LES-MINES.			No.2. SECTION. Amb. No. 11. Local work. Instruction of Ind division Indian Car. 72 wds. Ambulance Journey to BETHUNE. (General duty).	"
HOUCHAIN.			Amb. No. 14. Journey to VAUDRICOURT. (General duty)	"

WAR DIARY
or
INTELLIGENCE SUMMARY.

(Erase heading not required.) 15th Div F.M. Ambulance Workshop Unit No. 1 C.M.T.

Army Form C. 2118

Place	Date	Hour	Summary of Events and Information	Remarks and references to Appendices
HALLICOURT.	19/10/15	Tues.	(Cont.d) No. 3. SECTION Amb. No. 15. 40 a.b. (Officers 1 a spark). Amb. No. 17. 10 a.b. to Workshop. Amb. No. 17. 10 a.b. (Officers 1 a spark) Amb. No. 17. 3 Wet. Amb. No. 20. 30 a.b. (Ordnance stores + Officers 1 a spark).	B9. Wet. L.V.H.C.
NOEUX-LES-MINES	20/10/5	Wed.	WORKSHOP. No. 1. Sunbeam (No. 1 Self) taking down repairing radiator. Sunbeam car. Removing cylinders, cleaning pistons & cylinder heads, grinding in valves. 4 Ton petrol car carrier & hubs of 45th Field Ambulance.	1
NOEUX-LES-MINES			No. 1. SECTION. Amb. No. 2. Journey to VERNELLES & HALLICOURT, Amb. No. 4. Journey to URQUES. Amb. No. 6. Journey to LABEUVRIERE & "QUALITY" STREET Amb. No. 7. two journeys to HALLICOURT & one to LILLERS.	2
HOUCHAIN.			No. 2. SECTION. Amb. No. 14. About 40 miles for distribution of Sunbeam stores on wards.	1
HALLICOURT.			No. 3. SECTION. Amb. No. 16. 10 a.b. colliery. Amb. No. 20. 10 miles. Amb. No. 21. 12 a.b. for Medical Stores.	B. Wet. L.V.H.C.
NOEUX-LES-MINES	21/10/15	Thurs.	WORKSHOP Sunbeam Wkt. (No. 1 Self) taking down repairing radiator, & repairing canvas traveling, & painting wings & repairing broken ear. Adjusting exhibits magneto timing. Sunbeam No. 9. Painting wings & lamps (No. 2 Self). Ford No. 4. (No. 2 Self) Adjusting brakes. Fitting mystery height (Col. Johnson, No. Sec.) Repairing exhaust valve & type cable.	1
			No. 1. SECTION Amb. No. 3. Journey to LILLERS. Amb. No. 5. Journey to VIEUX-PETIT-SAINS. Amb. No. 7. two journeys to HALLICOURT, one to URQUES.	
NOEUX-LES-MINES			Amb. Nos. 2 & 3. moved to dressing station at VERNELLES. Amb. No. 3. two trips from VERNELLES to PHILOSOPHE, & one to NOEUX-LES-MINES.	
HOUCHAIN.			No. 2. SECTION A.A. No. 2. to colliery. M. A. 14. 10 journeys to VEVANT (Medical Stores). Amb. No. 14. No. Neaux-LES-MINES & ditto A.A. & No. N. 11 journeys to NOEUX-LES-MINES. Amb. 14. 10 Tea to BETHUNE.	
NOEUX-LES-MINES			No. 3. SECTION Charged Salim from HALLICOURT to NOEUX-LES-MINES. Amb. Nos. 15/6, 18, 21 6 a.b. No. 17, 12 a.b. for journeys. Charging Station. Amb. No. 16. 20. 16 a.b. Change Patients & collect.	B. Wet. L.V.H.C.

Army Form C. 2118

WAR DIARY
or
INTELLIGENCE SUMMARY.

(Erase heading not required.) 1st Dist of Motor Ambulance Convoy attached to 1st Army M.T.

Instructions regarding War Diaries and Intelligence Summaries are contained in F. S. Regs., Part II. and the Staff Manual respectively. Title pages will be prepared in manuscript.

Place	Date	Hour	Summary of Events and Information	Remarks and references to Appendices
NOEUX-LES-MINES	22/9/15	Aid.	WORKSHOP. Sunbeam No.10. Mtg'ris Centre fair & rear spring. Mories lorry A Coy new rear springs &c. Leaking petrol car arrived in vehicles of 47th Field Ambulance.	Col. E.L. Field
NOEUX-LES-MINES			No 1 SECTION. Ambs. Nos. 5 & 6. One journey to MAZINGARBE. No 1. Motor journeys to VERMELLES. Amb No.6. Journey to MAZINGARBE & ARQUES. Amb. No. 4. Journey to St. Pol.; escorting Amb No. 3 r 4. Six journeys from VERMELLES to PHILOSOPHE.	"
HOUCHIN			No 2 SECTION. Ambs. Nos. 9, 10 La Mothlque. Amb. M. 12. Journey to HALLICOURT & LILLERS. Amb. No. 14. Journey to LILLERS. Amb. Ebrouvin & LABUSSOY.	"
NOEUX-LES-MINES			No. 3 SECTION. Chubbi. Bearnley. Amb. No. 15. 32 cols. Amb. No. 16. 40 cols. Amb. No. 17. 42 cols. Amb. No. 18. 26 cols. Amb. No. 20. 66 cols. La Amb. No. 21. 20 cols for indices etc.	" ELRutter NAAC
NOEUX-LES-MINES	23/9/15	Sat.	WORKSHOP. Radys w/cyclic of FRANKLIN. No. 2 Scout Works of Nothing, new Back axle of frais. Brabel. Leaking filler flat. new rear carriers for 47th Field Ambulance Ambulance. A.Mg. r drilling plates for new tap. Saloon. Vauxhall TAIRE. 6 repairs. to D.M. Day N.	"
NOEUX-LES-MINES			No.1 SECTION. Amb. No. 2. Long journeys GUERNELLES. Amb. No. 4. Journey to LILLERS. Amb. No. 6. Journey to ROEUX = PETIT-SAINS. Amb. No. 1. Journeys to St. Pol r ARQUES.	"
VERMELLES			Ambs. Nos. 3 r 5. B run from VERMELLES to PHILOSOPHE & one journey from HULLOCH to PHILOSOPHE.	"
NOEUX-LES-MINES			No 2 SECTION. Amb. No. 8, 9. runs to NOEUX-LES-MINES & LILLERS. Amb No. 9. Journey to MARLES-LES-MINES. for Indices & Fritz. & Amb. No. 13. Journey to BARLIN.	"
NOEUX-LES-MINES			No. 3 SECTION. Bearnleybring Amb. No. 15. 18 cols. Amb. No. 16. 12 cols. Field No. 17. 28 cols. Amb. Mo. 18. 12 cols. Fild No. 1, 24 cols; Ambc. No. 18, 20 uphs. Amb. No. 20, 24 cols. J ½ or Local fireo.	" ELRutter NAAC

2353 Wt. W2544/1454 700,000 5/15 D. D. & L.   A.D.S.S. Forms/C. 2118.

WAR DIARY
or
INTELLIGENCE SUMMARY

Army Form C. 2118

(Erase heading not required.) 1st Div. Field Ambulance Workshop Unit

Place	Date	Hour	Summary of Events and Information	Remarks and references to Appendices
NOEUX-LES-MINES.	24/10/15	Sun	WORKSHOP. Ford/No.20. (No.1 Sect) Repairing generator, making petrol can carriers for No.2. Sect. An inlet non-return valve fitted (Sergt BOWER)(No.3 sect).	Details filled
			Forging new spring for back axle. Magneto (See Valve) down, rebearing engine. Sent to ST.OMER to generator & tail lamp rejecting leads.	
NOEUX-LES-VINES			No. 1 SECTION Amb. No.1. Transport Journey to VERMELLES. Amb.No.6 Journey to NOEUX-PETIT-SAINS. Amb.No.1. Journey to the Post.	
VERMELLES.			Amb. Mo. 8 & 15. Amb.No. 3. 6 journeys, No. 5. 7 journeys to PHILOSOPHE.	,,
HOUCHIN.			No. 2. SECTION. Amb.No. 10. 8 calls to theatre in the station. Amb.No. 14. Journey to BARLIN.	,,
NOEUX-LES-MINES			No.3 SECTION. Collecting Camera duty. Amb.No. 16. 2 pt Ca. Amb.No. 17. 2 cals. Amb.No. 20. 5 cals. Amb.No. 15. 12 cals. BB. Am. Tr. Wt. R.A.C.	,,
NOEUX-MINES.	25/10/15	Mon.	WORKSHOP. Sunbeam (No.1) Petrol car carrier. No. 2 Sect Sunbeam car. Bacouy brake down. Receiving brakes. Marine Eng. Lorry	
			ditch pin for two springs. Myself (No. 3 Sect) Removing hubs rebabbiting them. Myself (No.2 sect) All the new steering lead ball races.	
			Myself (No.1 sect) Dean anything in engine of motor valve.	
NOEUX-LES-MINES			No. 1 SECTION. Amb. No.6. Journey to NOEUX-PETIT-SAINS. ICQ. Amb. 6. 2 VERMELLES Amb. No.1. No. 2. Journey to VERMELLES. Amb.No. 4. Journey	
			to PHILOSOPHE. Amb. No. ? One Journey from VERMELLES & PHILOSOPHE Amb.No. 7 car to CHOCAVES. Amb.No.5. Five journeys from	
			VERMELLES & PHILOSOPHE, one to NOEUX-LES-MINES.	
HOUCHIN.			No. 2. SECTION. Amb.No. 10. Journey to ST.VENANT. General Duty.	
NOEUX-LES-MINES.			No.3. SECTION. General Collecting and Post Amb.No.15. 20 cals; Amb.No.16. 24 cals; Amb.No.17. 26 cals; Amb.No.20.24 cals; Amb.No. 21. 16 cals.	
			BB.Am.Tr.Wt. R.A.C.	
NOEUX-LES-MINES	26/10/15	Tues.	WORKSHOP. Picking petrol can carriers(No.2. Sect). Sunbeam car. Grinding up grooves making new stackgap cam bucking set etc	,,

WAR DIARY
or
INTELLIGENCE SUMMARY

(Erase heading not required.) 15th Div: XI Amb. [illegible]

Army Form C. 2118

Place	Date	Hour	Summary of Events and Information	Remarks and references to Appendices
NOEUX-LES-MINES.	28/10/15	—	WORKSHOP (cont) for No. 3 Sect. M/cycle (no 3 seat) tube, sparking plug, fab-pins rebuilt. M/cycle (no 1 seat) chain belting, engine refitted. Ambl. [illegible] new Radiator, carbs.	"
NOEUX-LES-MINES.			No.1 SECTION. Amb. No. 8 & 9 Journey to VERMELLES. Ambs. Nos. 6 & 7 Local Work. Amb. No. 7 Journey to ARQUES.	"
VERMELLES.			Amb. No. 3. Journey No. 5 & Journey to PHILOSOPHE.	"
HOUCHIN.			No. 2 SECTION. Amb. No. 14 Journey to VERMELLES.	"
NOEUX-LES-MINES.			No. 3 SECTION. Collecting Evac. Lying. Amb. No. 15. 36 cols. Amb. No. 17. 24 cols.; Amb. No. 20. 24 cols. Amb. No. 21. 20 cols. B.Sh. H. J.M.O.	"
NOEUX-LES-MINES.	27/10/15	Wed.	WORKSHOP. Making, fitting, strengthening piece on stating handle. Sunbeam Car. Fixing receiving dynamo in new position. M/cycle (No. 3 Seat) Lining new shackles & pins. (No. 2 Sec.) Forging, fitting pilot on carriers.	"
NOEUX-LES-MINES.			No.1 SECTION. Amb. No. 2. to HOCQUES. Amb. No. 4. to LA BASSEE, then to MOIRE, then to ARQUES. Amb. No. 3. then to ST. VENANT. Amb. No. 3. 4 runs. No. 5. 5 runs. from VERMELLES to PHILOSOPHE.	"
HOUCHIN.			No. 2 SECTION. Amb. No. 13. Journey to BETHUNE & NOEUX-LES-MINES. Amb. No. 14 to VERMELLES. Dassins.	"
NOEUX-LES-MINES.			No. 3 SECTION. Collecting & Evacuating Lying. Amb. No. 15. 3 cols.; Amb. No. 12. 28 cols. Amb. No. 18. 32 cols.; Amb. No. 20. 24 cols. Amb. No. 21. 33 cols. B.Sh. H.	"
NOEUX-LES-MINES	28/10/15	Thurs.	WORKSHOP. No. 2. Seat. busk in filling petrol car carriers. Sunbeam Car. Making platform easily & carefully. M/cycle (no. 3 seat). Signing up Lafs Press, Lamp Cycle (No. 1 seat) Making chain guard & tray. M/cycle (no 3 seat) Brazing carriers to Benins of Straton Box. Folio. M/c & & the Post.	"
			No. 1 SECTION. Amb. No. 7. Journey to NOEUX-PETIT-SANS, the Post, & LILLERS. Amb. No. 2. Run to ARQUES. Ambs. Nos. 3. & 4. Runs from VERMELLES to PHILOSOPHE.	"
NOEUX-LES-MINES.			to VERMELLES. Amb. No. 3. & 4. Runs & No. 5. 3 runs from VERMELLES to PHILOSOPHE.	"

Army Form C. 2118

WAR DIARY
or
INTELLIGENCE SUMMARY

(Erase heading not required.) /3 rd Div. Hd Qrs H. Motor Ambulance Workshop Unit A.S.C. M.T.

Place	Date	Hour	Summary of Events and Information	Remarks and references to Appendices
HOUCHIN.	28/10/15	Thurs	No 2 SECTION. Amb. No. 8, 9, 11 Local work. Amb. No. 14 Garage to BETHUNE & Workshops	Details Filed
NOEUX-LES-MINES.			No 3 SECTION Collecting Evacuating etc. Amb. No. 15, 32 n.l.s, No. 11, 16, 17, 12 n.l.s; No. 18, 20 n.l.s, No. 20, 4 n.l.s; No. 21, 16 n.l.s. General. Six drivers arrived & Workshops from Base M.T. Depôt, were distributed as per section.	B.E. Lutton M.A.S.C.
NOEUX-LES-MINES	29/10/15	Fri	WORKSHOP. Sunbeam Car forging & end fittings, Cast olepram pulley. (No 3 Sect) Issuing spring for brake. Issued SPARE to report to D.A.D.G.T.	"
NOEUX-LES-MINES			No 1 SECTION. Ambs Nos 3, 5, 6. Run to VERMELLES. Amb No. 6. Run to NOEUX-PETIT-SANS. Amb. No. 7 Local work. Run to LILLERS Ambs Nos 3 & 5. Three Runs to PHILOSOPHE then returned to NOEUX-LES-MINES.	"
VERMELLES.			No 2 SECTION. Amb. No. 8 Run to LILLERS. Amb. No. 12 Local for drivers instruction. Amb. No. 13. Runs to VERMELLES & LABUISSIERE.	"
HOUCHIN.			No 3 SECTION Evacuating. Amb. No. 15, 12 n.l.s. for instruction, No. 16, 24 n.l.s; No. 17, 24 n.l.s; No. 20, 24 n.l.s, No. 21, 8 n.l.s.	B.E. Lutton M.A.S.C.
NOEUX-LES-MINES.	30/10/15	Sat	WORKSHOP. Sunbeam Car Carby Pulley Ford No. 20 (No. 1 Sect) forging clip. H/eyed (No 3 sect) Turning resp pipe fine Sunbeam Car. forging hand fittings, hubing petrol can carrier (No 3 Sect)	"
NOEUX-LES-MINES			No 1 SECTION. Amb. No. 3. Run to ARQUES. Amb. No. 5. Run to VERMELLES. Amb. No. 6 Run to the posh. VERMELLES. Amb. No. y Runs to NOEUX-PETIT- SANS v to LABUISSIERE. Amb. No. 4. One run & Amb. No. 2. Six runs from VERMELLES to PHILOSOPHE	"
HOUCHIN.			No 2 SECTION Amb No. 9. Run to CHOCQUES. Amb. No. 10. Run 5 14 n.l.s for drivers instruction.	"
NOEUX-LES-MINES.			No 3 SECTION. Collecting Evacuating. Amb No. 16, 36 n.l.s, Amb No. 17, 24 n.l.s. Amb No. 20, 24 n.l.s. Amb. No. 21, 16 n.l.s offres transports.	B.E. Lutton Lt M.A.S.C.

Army Form C. 2118

WAR DIARY
or
~~INTELLIGENCE SUMMARY~~
(Erase heading not required.)

15th Divl. Field Ambulance Workshop Lieut. R.E.C.M.S.

Place	Date	Hour	Summary of Events and Information	Remarks and references to Appendices
NOEUX-LES-MINES	31/05/15	5am	**WORKSHOP.** Sunbeam Car. Repairing lamp bracket. Stove toying cable spring bolts for Sunbeam. Ford No.20 (No 2 Sect.) Fitting clip. Wolseley No.16 (No.3 Sect.) Removing cylinder friendling in valvts. Warrior lorry. Fitting new retain pin of pinol. Sunbeam Car. Repairing head lamp. Towed in Sunbeam No.2 from VERMELLES. Radiator damaged by shell fire during night.	Detail filed
MOEUX-LES-MINES			**No.1 SECTION** Amb. No.7. Run to NOEUX-PETIT-LANS. No.6. Run to MOYELLES. No.3. 3 y 7. Runs EVERMELLES. No.4. two runs to No.2. Five runs from VERMELLES to PHILDSOPHE.	"
HOUCHIN.			**No.2. SECTION** Amb. No.8. Run to CHOCQUES. No.12. Runs to NOEUX-LES-MINES & MAZINGARBE. No.13. 4 6 combdes to shell Pte PARKER. Transferred from R.T. Div. Safely Col. Farr.	"
MOEUX-LES-MINES			**No.3. SECTION.** Amb. No.15. 30 w.b. Officers & Medical Stores; No.16. 24 w.b. Beuvry & Fields; No.17. 24 w.b. Beuvry; No.18. 12 w.b. February No.14. No.20. 14 w.b. Cetherty & Beuvry; No.21. 16 w.b. transport duty.	"

B.B. Winton, Lt. R.E.C

15th F.A.N.U.
tot: 5

121/7656

15th Kuroun

Nov 15

Nov 1915 F

Army Form C. 2118

WAR DIARY
or
INTELLIGENCE SUMMARY.

(Erase heading not required.) 15th Div. Ft A.M.C. Advanced Workshop Unit A.S.C.

Instructions regarding War Diaries and Intelligence Summaries are contained in F. S. Regs., Part II. and the Staff Manual respectively. Title pages will be prepared in manuscript.

Place	Date	Hour	Summary of Events and Information	Remarks and references to Appendices
MEUX-LES-MINES.	1/11/15	Mon.	WORKSHOP Working on Sunbeam car, No 2 & Ford, Royce No 3 Lorry, Petrol car carried for No 3. Sect. No 1 & 3 Section Colliery evacuating No. 3. Section, no detail. B.E.F. Nth. U.A.A.C.	Dec. 31st old.
"	2/11/15	Tues.	Workshop Looking on Sunbeam car dynamo, Repaired No 3 sect, Peugeot, 2 Ford, 8 Stoke Typres. Sections No 1 & 3 Colliery evacuating, No 2 & 3. Taking Looking Parties up 6th trenches. B.E.F. Nth. U.A.A.C.	—
"	3/11/15	Wed.	Workshop working on Sunbeam Dynamo, No 4 Sunbeam, Starter in Store Lorry, No 19 Workshop, Douglas & Peugeot No 3 sect. Sections 1 & 3 Colliery & evacuating. No 2. No detail. B.E.F. Nth. U.A.A.C.	"
"	4/11/15	Thurs.	Workshop working on Sunbeam Nos. 10, 11, & 2. Fords Nos. 13, 14, 20 & 21. Workshop No 19. Motor cycle No 3 sect (Douglas) Assisted No. 10 Sunbeam for Hospital from Hersul Div. F.A.M.U. Sections Nos 1, 2 & 3 Colliery evacuating.	—
"	5/11/15	Fri.	Workshop Working on Hupmobile, No 2 Sunbeam, No 6 & 7 Ford Amb. Cars, Sunbeam Car, 2 & No 2 Sect. Rudge. Injured. Sections 1, 2 & 3 Colliery & Evacuating. B.E.F. Nth. U.A.A.C.	"
"	6/11/15	Sat.	Workshop Tracking new skid chains, & repairing Workshop stores. Working No 10 Hupmobile. No 19 Workshop, No 11 Sunbeam Ambulance, No 2 sect. Rudge m/cycle. Second to A.I.R.E. to report to D.D of D.T. Sections 1, 2 & 3 Colliery & Evacuating. B.E.F. Nth. U.A.A.C.	—
"	7/11/15	Sun.	Workshop Working on No 19 Workshop, Hupmobile, 8 Fords Nos. 6 & 7 Sections Colliery & evacuating. B.E.F. Nth. U.A.A.C.	"
"	8/11/15	Mon.	Workshop Work on Store Lorry, Skid chains, Workshop Stoke, Workshop (Part of) differential Shaft. Running carbon deposit of exhaust, Workshop Engine, Harris Living. All Sections evacuating & Colliery. B.E.F. Nth. U.A.A.C.	"
"	9/11/15	Tues.	Workshop Work on No 8 Workshop (Steering arm bent) Sunbeam Cars (detail). Austin engine & making spanners. Sections Colliery & evacuating. B.E.F. Nth. U.A.A.C.	"

Army Form C. 2118

WAR DIARY
or
INTELLIGENCE SUMMARY
(Erase heading not required.) 15th District ?/M/? Motor Lorry Workshop Unit Adv. M.T. 7

Instructions regarding War Diaries and Intelligence Summaries are contained in F.S. Regs., Part II. and the Staff Manual respectively. Title pages will be prepared in manuscript.

Place	Date	Hour	Summary of Events and Information	Remarks and references to Appendices
NOEUX-LES-MINES	10/11/15	Wed.	Workshop. Work on radiator fitting & valve dome (Rotoslug 19) Lamp (Rotoslug 17) Radiators (Sunbeams 1 & 2) Differential (Rotoslug No. 19) Valve Lifters, footboards (Auto Cycle. Col. Wolseley) Lamp brackets (Sunbeam car) Sections collecting & repairing.	B.Blatter ?/7/?/A.C. D.B.? Lt. Col
"	11/11/15	Thurs.	Workshop. Engine cleaning (Sunbeam 4) Painting & testing 4/6 (Sunbeam 2) Stripping new tyre (Ford 2) Differential (Rotoslug 19) Valve cam (Applying) to 1 Car, 1 Lorry (Signal Co), 1 Lorry (Sanitary Section) started to load for repairs by 6 Corps letter No. S527/6. of 9/11/15. Sections collecting & repairing. Mech. Staff. Sergt CUTTER went to England for on leave till 21/11/15.	B.Blatter ?/7/?/A.C.
"	12/11/15	Fri.	Workshop. Work on axle (Sunbeam 4) Radiator & cylinder plugs (Rotoslug 19) Valve cap (Wolseley) Sections collecting & repairing.	B.Blatter ?/7/?/A.C.
"	13/11/15	Sat.	Workshop. Fabricating Sunbeams (46 F.E.A.) & Ford test boxes. Issued & repaired to D.D.G.T. & to R.E. Sections collecting & repairing.	B.Blatter ?/7/?/A.C.
"	14/11/15	Sun.	Workshop. Work on cylinder Spanner (41 F.E.A.) Testing & taking down engine (Div. Hd. Qr. tenders) No. 1 Shed (46th F.A. moved from NOEUX-LES-MINES to HESDIGNEUL, 48th F.A. moved from HOUCHIN to NOEUX-LES-MINES. All sections collecting & repairing.	B.Blatter ?/7/?/A.C.
"	15/11/15	Mon.	WORKSHOP. Mudguard & test Box (Sunbeam car) Engine ground overhaul (Sunbeam S.S.O.) testing & spanners (46 F.E.A.) Sections collecting & repairing.	B.Blatter ?/7/?/A.C.
"	16/11/15	Tues.	WORKSHOP. Working frames for bearers, testing new lorry (Sunbeam 5) Accumulator (Workshop Sunbeam) Brake (Singer 15th Sig. Co.) Lagonda (Sunbeam I.S.O.) Sections collecting & repairing.	B.Blatter ?/7/?/A.C.
"	17/11/15	Wed.	WORKSHOP. Work on skid chains for Harris. Lamp brackets (No. 13 Ford). Back axle & springs (Singer Signal Co.) Mudguards, tyre pump & testing (Sunbeam S.S.O.) Rear Spring (Sunbeam M.9841. Div. Train). Sections collecting & repairing.	B.Blatter ?/7/?/A.C.
"	18/11/15	Thurs.	WORKSHOP. Work on type (Ford Lords Nos. 13 & 14). Skid chains (Harris) Differential (Rotoslug 19) Turning differential shaft (Singer Signal) Rear Spring (Sunbeam M.9841. Div. Train) Adjusting Magneto (Sunbeam M.14482. S.S.O.) Sections collecting & repairing.	B.Blatter ?/7/?/A.C.

Army Form C. 2118

WAR DIARY
or
INTELLIGENCE SUMMARY

(Erase heading not required.) 15th Divl. Sigl. Coy. Ln Lanc. Workshop Sect. A.C.M.T.

Instructions regarding War Diaries and Intelligence Summaries are contained in F. S. Regs., Part II. and the Staff Manual respectively. Title pages will be prepared in manuscript.

Place	Date	Hour	Summary of Events and Information	Remarks and references to Appendices
NOEUX-LES-MINES	19/11/15	Fri.	WORKSHOP. Work on differential (Wolseley 19) Genus & hub caps (workshop Sunbeam) Coil covers & timing differential chap 1 (Cooper Signal Co.) CCHS 2 Dr Col. Fld. door Lock, examination. (Sunbeam M9209. Div.Train) Tyring testing (Sunbeam M1448Z. S.S.O.) Sections collecting & evacuating. B.Dutton S/S K.C.	
"	20/11/15	Sat.	WORKSHOP. Work on test brake (Rd. 6) Tyres & lamps. (Sunbeam No. 2) Examination (Adjustment etc) having different shafts fitting windscreen (10 P Signal Co.) Tuning engine (Sunbeam M 1448Z. S.S.O.) Sections collecting & evacuating. Inspected to D.O./S/S. & staff & Dey B.Dutton S/S K.C.	
"	21/11/15	Sun.	WORKSHOP. Work on Sunbeam (workshop) Coil covers. Radiator Sunbeam (No. 3) Differentials & screen (Cooper Signal Co.) Springs Trailer (Sunbeam M 9829. Div.Train) Adjusting lights & clutch cover (Sunbeam M1448Z. S.S.O.) Sections Collecting & evacuating. B.Dutton S/S K.C.	
"	22/11/15	Mon.	WORKSHOP. Work on differentials, gear box & front spring (Cooper Signal Co.) Spring, Photo truck & mudguards (Sunbeam M 9829 Div.Train) Dismantling engine & having whang old flywheel. (Sunbeam M 9840. Div.Train) Repairing wheels. (Douglas m/cycle No. 2 Sect.) Sections collecting & evacuating. B.Dutton S/S K.C.	
"	23/11/15	Tue.	WORKSHOP. Packing castle spring & spring hitch. Setting up & & spring leaves (Sunbeam No. 2.) Repairing accumulators (workshop Sunbeam) Fitting clip (Rd. No. 21) Repairing carrier (Rudge m/cycle 2 sect). Sections & supp r mudguards. (Sunbeam M 9840. Div.Train) Sections Collecting & evacuating. B.Dutton S/S K.C.	
"	24/11/15	Wed.	WORKSHOP. Work on skid chain & shutters. Fitting new rear springs (Stoddalls No. 20121) Work on clutch, cylinder & windshield (Sunbeam Div.Train Lighting set (workshop Sunbeam). Sections Collecting & evacuating. B.Dutton S/S K.C.	
"	25/11/15	Thurs.	WORKSHOP. Work on wind screen fittings (workshop Sunbeam) Mudguards etc (Sunbeam M 9829. Div.Train) Skid chains for Karrier. B.Dutton S/S K.C.	
"	"	"	Section No. 2 moved to LABOURSE. All Sections collecting & evacuating.	
GOSNAY.	26/11/15	Fri.	WORKSHOP. Workshop moved to school-yard at GOSNAY. Sections collecting & evacuating. B.Dutton S/S K.C.	
"	27/11/15	Sat.	WORKSHOP. Adjusting & fitting selector rods (Karrier) Work on springs (Sunbeam No. 2) Hub (Sunbeam M1483 Div.Train) Clutch & cable (Rudge No. 2 sect) Dynamo Exhaust valve & tyre cable (Douglas m/cycle No. 2 Sect). No. 1. Section moved to VERQUIGNEUL. Sections all collecting & evacuating. B.Dutton S/S K.C.	

Army Form C. 2118.

WAR DIARY
or
INTELLIGENCE SUMMARY.

(Erase heading not required.)

15th Div - Mobile Workshop Humboldt Unit, RAMC M.T.

Instructions regarding War Diaries and Intelligence Summaries are contained in F. S. Regs., Part II. and the Staff Manual respectively. Title pages will be prepared in manuscript.

Place	Date	Hour	Summary of Events and Information	Remarks and references to Appendices
GOSNAY	29/11/15	Sun.	WORKSHOP. Repairing burst radiator tubing near mudguards (Ford No.20) & rind screen (workshop Sunbeam) Removing cylinders of car being cast in a big jacket (Sunbeam M9834 Div. Train) had to get bit chain gear box. Seized collecting security.	B.E. Sutton A.S.C.
"	29/11/15	Mon.	WORKSHOP. Work on valves, cylinders, rocker arm of (Sunbeam No. M9839 Div Train) Brakes (Ford No. 4436) Radiator & mudguards (Ford No.20) Crank spring bolt (Sunbeam No.5.Tilling 2 windscreens, wheel bearings, breaks (Sunbeam M209 Div.Train). Inspected all the ambulances with Ast. Staff Serg CUTLER at NOEUX-LES-MINES, PHILOSOPHE, VERMELLES, LABOURSE, VERQUINSNEUR, SAINS & the lorry recently.	B.E. Sutton A.S.C.
"	30/11/15	Tues.	WORKSHOP. Work on radiators & wings (Ford No. 20) Rear Spring (Horse) rubs & chains (Kerry) Jack & coils cylinder tappets (Coy). Sent to Ordnance dept M. NOEUX-LES-MINES for worn Ford MC.Oil cans. Sates & the lorry recently.	B.E. Sutton A.S.C.

15ᵗʰ P.a.w.v.
Vol. 6

121/7809

15ᵗʰ Hurcum

Dec 1905

Koch 15

WAR DIARY
or
INTELLIGENCE SUMMARY.

Army Form C. 2118.

(Erase heading not required.) 15th Divl. Supply Column Workshop Unit R.F.C.

Instructions regarding War Diaries and Intelligence Summaries are contained in F. S. Regs., Part II. and the Staff Manual respectively. Title pages will be prepared in manuscript.

Place	Date	Hour	Summary of Events and Information	Remarks and references to Appendices
GOSNAY	1/12/15	Wed.	WORKSHOP Work on brake rod (Singer 15th Tynd. Co. R.E.) Valve to flat standpipe (Infy cyls. No. 2 sect.) Removing carbon deposits, grinding in valves	Detail filed
"	2/12/15	Thurs.	(Co. 7 Ford.) Fitting new wind screen (Workshop Sunbeam) Shield chains (Warrior) Section collecting, remainder WORKSHOP Work on door lock (Rolls-Royce) Spindle to exh. lead pipe (Workshop Sunbeam) Lock fitted (Co. 2 Ford) Making cutters (Workshop). Repairing old bracket (Warrior) Fitting footrests to the (Infy cyls. No. 2 sect.) Section collecting, remainder	B.S. Hutton Lt. R.F.C. B.S. Hutton Lt. R.F.C.
"	3/12/15	Frid.	WORKSHOP Work on shield chains (Warrior) Taking up spring pins on infy cyls. kit sect. Section collecting, remainder	B.S. Hutton Lt. R.F.C.
"	4/12/15	Sat.	WORKSHOP Work on spring clip, nipping (Singer 15th Cp. R.E.) Fitting new steering tie-rod (Workshop Sunbeam) Repairing two new spring brasses (Workshop Sunbeam) Mending oft pain tank (Workshop Sunbeam) Repltg. fire Extinguisher, 15th & 17th Infy. Section collecting, remainder	B.S. Hutton Lt. R.F.C.
"	5/12/15	Sun.		B.S. Hutton Lt. R.F.C.
"	6/12/15	Mon.	WORKSHOP took a break fulls kup continue "Esforzado" (the 15 Lt. Horley & No. 3 Sunbeam) fitting woods to Workshop officers side with lamps, turning cutting punches (Workshop). Section collecting, remainder.	B.S. Hutton Lt. R.F.C.
"	7/12/15	Tues.	WORKSHOP Removing carbon deposit from cylinders & pistons grinding in valves, refacing crank case, body-main guards (Sunbeam M9841. Division) fitting safe guards to tappets (Workshop Inch), sent R.A.V.C. HEL to work for repairs of workshop. Section collecting, remainder	B.S. Hutton Lt. R.F.C.
"	8/12/15	Wed.	WORKSHOP Work on Sunbeam kty engine, brakes, magneto, tappets, tappet guides, grease cup injector, overhaul (Sunbeam M9941.15th Division), taking down cylinders, removing carbon deposit grinding in valves, fitting new rear spring ends to (Sunbeam amb. No. 12.) Section collecting, remainder	B.S. Hutton Lt. R.F.C.
"	9/12/15	Thurs.	WORKSHOP took a Brakes, three arm, break down, irons. (Sunbeam M9941 15th Division) Taking down cylinders, removing carbon deposit refacing grinding in valves, packing & fitting new running board repairing mudguards (Sunbeam VI. 9205.15th Divl. Training) Working in workshop in Society Shed. No. IX.	B.S. Hutton Lt. R.F.C.

Army Form C. 2118.

WAR DIARY
or
INTELLIGENCE SUMMARY. 15th Divl Field Ambulance Workshop Unit A.S.C.

(Erase heading not required.)

Instructions regarding War Diaries and Intelligence Summaries are contained in F.S. Regs., Part II. and the Staff Manual respectively. Title pages will be prepared in manuscript.

Place	Date	Hour	Summary of Events and Information	Remarks and references to Appendices
GOSNAY	9/12/15	Thurs	(contd) dismantling engine & transferring track axle to No.19 lorry. Sections collecting renewing. B.E.Hutton S/Sgt A.S.C.	Details filed
GOSNAY.	10/12/15	Frid.	WORKSHOP. Assembling engine & overhauling car. Sunbeam M.9209 (15th Divl Train). Dismantling engine & removing same from frame. (No 17.) (lorry) Testing & tuning up of engine (No.19 lorry) Sections Collecting & renewing. B.E.Hutton S/Sgt A.S.C.	"
"	11/12/15	Sat.	WORKSHOP. Adjusting brakes & fitting new running board (Sunbeam M.9209, 15th Divl Train) Dismantling engine (No.17 lorry) Examining & adjusting brakes & retaining fitting bolts to easy stay, fitting new front spring centre bolt (workshop Sunbeam), Adjusting footbrake rectifying lamp bracket & journal to SIRE to report to D.D.of V.S. Sections Collecting & renewing. B.E.Hutton S/Sgt A.S.C.	"
"	12/12/15	Sun.	WORKSHOP. Fitting new fuel spring rear brake drum (Sunbeam M.9829, 15th Divl Train). Letting new distance piece to rear brake shoes (workshop Sunbeam) Dismantling Engine & bedding in crankshaft. (Probably No.17) Sections collecting & renewing. B.E.Hutton S/Sgt A.S.C.	"
"	13/12/15	Mon.	WORKSHOP. Turning & refitting oil retainer "safeguards" (Sunbeam 5.0.). Fitting new rear spring centre bolts (W&S.S. Sunbeam). Fitting foot brake & refitting running board (Sunbeam M.14482, 15th Divl Train). Redding in crank shaft (No.17 lorry) Turning & fitting Sunbeam spring centre bolts for stock. No 3. Section moved from NOEUX-LES-MINES to AUCHEL. All sections collecting, renewing etc. Journal to LILLERS to arrange for site for workshop till M.G. B.E.Hutton S/Sgt A.S.C.	"
"	14/12/15	Tues	WORKSHOP. Taking off cylinder heads, cleaning off carbon deposit, grinding in valves, adjusting spark timing etc. (No.7 Ford) Letting new springs, fitting new centre pins (W.&.J. Sunbeam). Fitting crank case in chassis (No.19 lorry) Fitting new front spring centre bolt (workshop Sunbeam), Turning up engine & fitting back of M/C (Ford No.20). No.1. Section moved to ALLOUAGNE from VERQUIGNEUL. All sections collecting & renewing. Journal to LILLERS re provisional workshop for workshop etc. B.E.Hutton S/Sgt A.S.C.	"

Army Form C. 2118.

WAR DIARY
or
INTELLIGENCE SUMMARY.

(Erase heading not required.) 15th Divl. Field Workshop Workshop Unit A.S.C.

Instructions regarding War Diaries and Intelligence Summaries are contained in F. S. Regs., Part II. and the Staff Manual respectively. Title pages will be prepared in manuscript.

Place	Date	Hour	Summary of Events and Information	Remarks and references to Appendices
LILLERS	15/12/15	Wed.	WORKSHOP Workshop moved from GOSNAY to LILLERS. Sections Nos 1 & 2 General duty No 3. Collecting Unservlg.	B&Ltn W.A.S.C. Detail field
LILLERS	16/12/15	Thurs.	WORKSHOP Unpacking arranging Camp at LILLERS. Section resting.	B&Ltn W.A.S.C. "
LILLERS.	17/12/15	Fri.	WORKSHOP Taking down cylinder heads, removing carbon deposit, grinding in valves, rebushing tie rod pins (Fords Nos 2, 5 & 6). Taking down cylinder heads, grinding in valves vauxhall Coy (No 9 Sunbeam) Forging, fitting studs & nuts for oil sump (No 9 Sunbeam). Section Collecting General Duty. Took Sunbeam Car M.1022 to Alippo 15th Corps received in exchange Wolseley M.1461. B&Ltn W.A.S.C. "
LILLERS.	18/12/15	Sat.	WORKSHOP Replacing cylinder heads. Finishing tie rod pins Fords (Ford Nos. 2, 1 & 6). Night Lining front wing, etc (Mo. 2 Sunbeam), Overhaulg lighting set & sandguards. Taking off cylinders (Probably totally) No 2 Sect. No detail. Nos. 1 & 3 General duty.	B&Ltn W.A.S.C. "
LILLERS.	19/12/15	Sun.	WORKSHOP Refixing footbrake (No 20 Ford). Dismantling Engine & concetly body Workshop totally). Overhaulg engine, taking up big ends, Refixing Carriers front mudguards (Daylur Argyle Col. Johnson). No. 2 Sect. No detail. Nos. 2 & 3 Generalduty B&Ltn W.A.S.C. "
LILLERS.	20/12/15	Mon.	WORKSHOP Taking down cylinders, removing carbon deposit, grinding in valves taking down driving shaft (No 8 Sunbeam), Fitg rear axle spring pin. (No 3 Sunbeam) Fitting new distance pin to brake lever (Sunbeam M.1482. 15th Divn. train.) Fitting connecty rod to crank shaft. Workshop totally. No. 17 Workshop totally. Section Collecting General duty.	B&Ltn W.A.S.C. 2
LILLERS.	21/12/15	Tues	WORKSHOP Taking off cylinders, grinding in valves (No 11 Sunbeam). Grinding in valves, fitting connectg rods (workshop totally taking them Examining gear box (Karrier Lorry) Burety engine (No 17 workshop). Taking down reverlantly magnets. Cleaner. Synenery, (Staff Signals Car) Changing gear box cluctech (R.S.H. w/g clutch Bugl. BOWLER). Sections No. 2. No detail. Nos 1 & 3. Collectg General duty. B&Ltn W.A.S.C.	"
LILLERS	22/12/15	Wed.	WORKSHOP Fitting tappet pins & valves (workshop totally) Dismantling gear box (Karrier Lorry) Burety engine (No 17 Workshop)	"

WAR DIARY or INTELLIGENCE SUMMARY

Army Form C. 2118.

15th Div'l - H.Q. Ambulance Workshop Unit A.S.C.

Place	Date	Hour	Summary of Events and Information	Remarks and references to Appendices
LILLERS.	22/12/15	Wed.	WORKSHOP Removed & fitting up 1 new spring clip of Sunbeam M983465 Div train. Warming jets per fire broke. (workshop lorry) Daimler field Despatched Daimler Car M747 Signal (Co.) to 3rd A.S.C. Repair shops G.H.Q. Grey ambulance from each section out 6/12th Div for 3 days. Section doing little collecting.	B.B.Walton Lt A.S.C.
LILLERS.	23/12/15	Thurs.	WORKSHOP Erecting engine of workshop "A" No 17 (workshop) Dismantling engine & removing fan from steam's sticky down crack. (No 21 Ford). Repairing mudguards of Thornycroft per (workshop lorry) Sections collecting generally.	B.B.Walton Lt A.S.C.
LILLERS.	24/12/15	Fri.	WORKSHOP Erecting cylinders (No 11 workshop) Repairing clutch & erecting engine (No 21 Ford) Putting mudguards etc (workshop lorry) Putting up gantries & making toggy hooks & tackle for dead Sd hops. Section generally.	B.B.Walton Lt A.S.C.
LILLERS.	25/12/15	Sat.	WORKSHOP Fitting engine in chassis of No 17 (workshop) No 21 Ford) Loading lorries & going on to work at Railhead & despatching to 2 A.S.C. Repair shops ROUEN. Fitting fan belt (No 68 Sunbeam). Section little general duty.	B.B.Walton Lt A.S.C.
LILLERS.	26/12/15	Sun.	WORKSHOP Assembling engine (No 17 workshop) Cleaning & packing up parts (No 17 workshop) hunting spanners for workshop use. Section 12. No detail Nos 1 & 3 collecting general duty.	B.B.Walton Lt A.S.C.
LILLERS.	27/12/15	Mon.	WORKSHOP Taking down & cleaning engine of torts 13 & 14). Repairing mudguards & removing & fitting lamp "safeguards" (No 18 Ford) Fitting up safeguards (No 14 Ford). Fitting new fan belt & shaft ball race & repairing door lock (Sunbeam M9540. 3rd Div Train). Erecting Radiator etc (No 17 workshop) Section collecting general duty.	B.B.Walton Lt A.S.C.
LILLERS	28/12/15	Tues	WORKSHOP Overhauling body fitting "safeguards" to side lamps (No 1 Ford) Examining rear hub & fitting side lamp "safeguards" & new spring adjusting engine etc (No 14 workshop) making castors & no lights. Section collecting general duty.	B.B.Walton Lt A.S.C.

1577 Wt.W10791/1773 500,000 1/15 D.D.&L. A.D.S.S./Forms/C. 2118.

Army Form C. 2118.

WAR DIARY
or
INTELLIGENCE SUMMARY.

(Erase heading not required.) 15th Divl — Lizdd Ambulance Workshops Units A.S.C

Instructions regarding War Diaries and Intelligence Summaries are contained in F. S. Regs., Part II. and the Staff Manual respectively. Title pages will be prepared in manuscript.

Place	Date	Hour	Summary of Events and Information	Remarks and references to Appendices
LILLERS.	29/12/15	Wed.	WORKSHOP. Fitting spring clip to rear stud. 1 M/Cycle (Cpl. JOHNSON). Renewing cylinders, cleaning off deposit, grinding in valves, fitting "Low" cylinder on running boards (two 15" cwt lorrys) (No 2 Sunbeam). Dismantling & fitting axle from No. 17 cwt lorry, fitting same to workshop lorry to replace one broken. Making & fitting cowls to seat lamps. Sent to KAIRE & total L.G.O.C. 30 cwt lorry to replace KARRIER. Sections Collecting & doing general duties.	Detail attached. Belletin N.T.A.C.
LILLERS.	30/12/15	Thurs	WORKSHOP. Taking off cylinders, removing carbon deposit, grinding in valves (No 3 Sunbeam), Renewing & adjusting (No 3 Sunbeam). Side brake rod (No. 7 Ford). Fitting cowls over side lamps & auxiliary brackets. (Nos 1, 2 & 3 Sections). All Sections Short runs collecting & local general duties.	,, Belletin N.T.A.C.
LILLERS.	31/12/15	Frid.	WORKSHOP. Fitting two new oil front springs, 4 shackle pins, 2 new front wheel ball races, making & fitting new shackle pin bushes. (Sunbeam M9839 15 cwt lorry). Removing cylinders, cleaning off carbon deposit, fitting new oil side valve spring cap in bolt. (No 1 Sunbeam) Fitting 2 new head lamps & brackets, 2 front wings. (Sunbeam No. 14482. 15th Divisional Supply Column spring forks, fitting chain guard, safety chain (Douglas M/Cycle. L/C-CPL JAMES). Sections General duties.	,, Belletin N.T.A.C.

15th F.A. W.V.
Vol: 7

F

January 1916

Army Form C. 2118.

WAR DIARY
~~INTELLIGENCE SUMMARY.~~

(Erase heading not required.) 15th Div. Mobile Ambulance Workshop Unit. A.S.C.

Instructions regarding War Diaries and Intelligence Summaries are contained in F.S. Regs, Part II. and the Staff Manual respectively. Title pages will be prepared in manuscript.

Place	Date	Hour	Summary of Events and Information	Remarks and references to Appendices
LILLERS. WORKSHOP	1916			
	Jan 1/16	Sat.	WORKSHOP. Working on footbrake (Ford No 20). Springs, front wheels & mudguards (Sunbeam M.T. 9839 15th Division). Repairing Lamps. Section. No.1. General duty. No.2. As detail. No.3. Collecting & evacuating.	Detail filed B. Hutton Lt. A.S.C.
"	2-1-'16	Sunday	WORKSHOP. Refixing rear wheels (Studebaker Lynx lorry 7974. 15th Div Signal Co.) Work on Engine & front brake drum (Ford No. 6.) Collecting & despatching unserviceable tyres to Base. Section. Collecting, Evacuating General duty.	Detail filed B. Hutton Lt. A.S.C.
"	3-1-16	Mon.	WORKSHOP. Refitting rear wheels (Studebaker Lynx lorry 7974. 15th Div Signal Co.) Overhauling engine (Sunbeam No.5.) Assembling engine (Ford No.6) Fitting mudspring centre bolt (workshop lorry) Section. Collecting, Evacuating General duty.	Detail filed B. Hutton Lt. A.S.C.
"	4-1-'16.	Tues.	WORKSHOP. Work on brake rod heads (Ford No. 20). Work on tappets, tyres & flywheel (Sunbeam No. 4. Sunbeam). Refixing clutch (No.1. Ford). Rear wheels (Studebaker-Lynx 7974. Signal Co.) Repairing back axle & fixing workshop car to station & despatching	Detail filed B. Hutton Lt. A.S.C.
"	5-1-16	Wed.	WORKSHOP. Work on clutch (No.7 Ford). Running board (lorry by M. T. 4061) Lynx (Sunbeam 9840. Div Train. Dist Exercise. Section General Duty & Dist Exercise.	Detail filed B. Hutton Lt. A.S.C.
"	6-1-16	Thurs	WORKSHOP. Overhauling Crank, workshop engine & tools. Fitting new fan. Belt (Highbstilt No.10). Section. Collecting, Evacuating and Dist Exercise	Detail filed B. Hutton Lt. A.S.C.
"	7-1-16	Frid.	WORKSHOP. Properly rebacing engine (Daimler lorry Lam. Sec.) Took a strain & work to fix hooks (Douglas motorcycle Sec.) Rocking up engine (No.6 Ford) Packing dynamo (workshop). Section. Collecting & evacuating Dist Exercise.	Detail filed B. Hutton Lt. A.S.C.

WAR DIARY
or
INTELLIGENCE SUMMARY

Army Form C. 2118.

(Erase heading not required.) 15th Div: Field Ambulance Workshop Unit

Place	Date	Hour	Summary of Events and Information	Remarks and references to Appendices
LILLERS	8/1/16	Sat.	WORKSHOP. Work on engine (Daimler lorry, Sun-beam Sec.1). Springs & mudguards (Sunbeam No.12.) Springs & mudguards (Sunbeam M.9840. Dist:Train) Safety lamp brackets (L.G.O.C. Lorry). Dist=Exercise indo. Sections General duty, etc. Casualty nil	B.Sutton E.R.S.C.
LILLERS	9/1/16	Sun.	WORKSHOP. Work on steering & working torpedo-support (Shaker-Guide Lorry, Sig.Co.) Took on & spring rebuilt (Sunbeam M.9840. Dist:Train) Engine (Daimler lorry, San. Sec.) Footwheel ballrace (No.6 Sunbeam) Sections General Duty	B.Sutton E.R.S.C.
LILLERS	10/1/16	Mon	WORKSHOP Work on Tarpaulin frame & lining (Khaki-Equivalory, Sig.Co.) Chiesel (Sunbeam M.9840. Dist:Train) Engine & Transmission (Ford No.20) Spring (Sunbeam M.14482 Dist:Tran.) Controls (Douglas m/cycle) Footbrake (Intersely M.1461) Sections General Duty.	B.Sutton E.R.S.C.
LILLERS	11/1/16	Tues	WORKSHOP. Work on Tarpaulin frame & lining (Khaki-Guide Lorry, Sig.Co.) Bodywork & springs (Sunbeam M.14482 Dist:Train) Engine, Carbs, & Transmission (Ford No.20) Controls (Douglas m/cycle) Sections General Duty.	B.Sutton E.R.S.C.
LILLERS	12/1/16	Wed.	WORKSHOP. Lorry in Sunbeam M.9639 (15th Div: Train) & dismantling differential. Work on springs & shafts (Sunbeam M.14482 Dist:Train) Fitting new brake drum (Sunbeam No.12.) Controls (Douglas m/cycle No.1 Sec.) Making new spring centre-pins & working on pin for overhauling fatter brakes (Hupmobile No.10). Sections General duty.	B.Sutton E.R.S.C.
LILLERS	13/1/16	Thurs.	WORKSHOP. Work on rear springs, fitting new cross wheel & fixing gear chains (Sunbeam M.9834. Dist:Train) Making jiffy arm spring lever (Sunbeam No.2) Sec:Train No.3. Fixed to Noeux-les-Mines, No.1 & 2 General Duty.	B.Sutton E.R.S.C.
LILLERS	14/1/16	Fri.	WORKSHOP Work on springs & axles (Hupmobile No.10) Hind springs (Sunbeam M.9889. Dist:Train) Heavy Engine (Ford No.6) Examining gears (Daimler M.395. Sig:Co.) Sections No.1 Guard to Noeux-les-Mines, No.2. General Duty. No.3. Colliery. Casualty.	B.Sutton E.R.S.C.

1577 Wt. W10791/1773 500,000 1/15 D.D. & L. A.D.S.S./Forms/C. 2118.

Army Form C. 2118.

WAR DIARY
or
INTELLIGENCE SUMMARY.

(Erase heading not required.) 3rd Div. Field Ambulance Workshop Unit A.S.C.

Place	Date	Hour	Summary of Events and Information	Remarks and references to Appendices
LILLERS				
NOEUX-LES-MINES	15/1/16	Sat.	WORKSHOP. Work on Springs (Hupmobile No.10) Packing up & moving to NOEUX-LES-MINES. Lieut. B.E. SUTTON proceeded to ENGLAND on 10 days detail fld. Adv. Section. No.1 General Duty. Nos. 2 & 3. Collecting & Evacuating.	B.Shelton S/Sgt A.S.C.
NOEUX-LES-MINES	16/1/16	Sun.	WORKSHOP. Tuning up Engine (Ford No.20). Rear Spring (Hupmobile No.10). Cleaning Lorries & Camp. Letting Collecting & Evacuating.	B.Shelton S/Sgt A.S.C.
"	17/1/16	Mon.	WORKSHOP. Workshop on Engine & dynamo (Ford No.6.) Spring of Hupmobile No.10.) Brake (Douglas m/cycle No.1. Sec.) Engine raising (Ford No.20.) Workshop Ambulance No. A.17664 arrived to replace No.17 Workshop (6.cyl Wolseley No. 17). Section 24-30 P. Workshop Ambulance No A.17664 arrived to replace No.17 Workshop and 1st Section Collecting & Evacuating.	B.Shelton S/Sgt A.S.C.
"	18/1/16	Tues.	WORKSHOP Work on Mudguards (L.G.O.C. lorry) Engine Dynamo rebuild (Ford No.6.) Setting of fifty Brakebolts, took to side lamps (6.cyl. Wolseley No.17). Brake control (Douglas m/cycle No.3. Sec.). Setting (Wolseley M.1461). Section Collecting Evacuating.	B.Shelton S/Sgt A.S.C.
"	19/1/16	Wed.	WORKSHOP. Work on Engine (Ford No.6.) Rear Springs (Sunbeam No.5.) Steering steering gear chains (Wolseley M.1461) Work on Springs, axle, &c, Painting car (Sunbeam M.14482. Div. Train.) Mudguard Stays (L.G.O.C. lorry) Letting No.9 Gun workshop. 2 & 3. Collecting & Evacuating.	B.Shelton S/Sgt A.S.C.
"	20/1/16	Thurs.	WORKSHOP. Work on Steering &c (Wolseley M.1461) Mudguard Stays (L.G.O.C lorry) Side Brake (Sunbeam No.4.) Painting Staining Sunbeam M.1440. Dist. Train.) Section Collecting & Evacuating.	B.Shelton S/Sgt A.S.C.
"	21/1/16	Fri.	WORKSHOP Work on Steering (Wolseley M.1461) Mudguard Stays (L.G.O.C. Lorry) Painting Sunbeam M.14482 Div.Train). Sections Collecting & Evacuating. Bde A.S.C.	B.Shelton S/Sgt A.S.C.
"	22/1/16	Sat.	WORKSHOP Tuning up Whaler (Wolseley M.1461.) Repairing pedals of lift cab (Ford No.20.) Painting Sunbeam M.14482 Div.Division). Sections No.1 General Duty. Nos. 2 & 3. Collecting & Evacuating.	B.Shelton S/Sgt A.S.C.
"	23/1/16	Sun.	WORKSHOP. Work on front wheel rains (Ford No.6.) Six not from Medical front attached No.10 Repairing wheel spanned Wolseley Ambulance No.3. Sec.)	

WAR DIARY
or
INTELLIGENCE SUMMARY.

Army Form C. 2118.

(Erase heading not required.) 15th Divl Supply Column Ammunition Park A.S.C.

Place	Date	Hour	Summary of Events and Information	Remarks and references to Appendices
NOEUX-LES-MINES	24/1/16	Sun.	WORKSHOP. Overhauling engine (Sunbeam M.9834. Div.Train). Staring pinion (Ford No.20). Repairing spring (Ford No.20). Section No.1 Collecting. Section No.1 General duty. Nos.2 & 3 Collecting and evacuating. Two cars No.1 Section collecting, evacuating from PHILOSOPHE. B.Echelon N.T.A.S.C.	
"	25/1/16	Mon.	WORKSHOP. Work on Engine (Sunbeam M.9834. Div.Train), Ford shut ball races Front Lock (Sunbeam M.1841. Div.Train), Hub Cap. (Sunbeam No.12). Brake (Rudge b/cycle No.1 Sect.) Staring (Ford No.21.) Section Nos 1 & 3 General duty Collecting, Evacuating. No.2 Collecting Evacuating. B.Echelon N.T.A.S.C.	
"	26/1/16	Tues.	WORKSHOP. Work on Springs (Sunbeam M.9209 Div Train.) Springs front wheel ball races (Sunbeam M.999 Div Train.) Straightening staring tie-rod (Sunbeam No.12.) Repairing rear wing (Sunbeam No.8.) Dismantling engine (Ford No.20) Section Collecting, Evacuating General duty. B.Echelon N.T.A.S.C.	
"	27/1/16	Wed.	WORKSHOP. took a Engine, coils & dynamo (Ford No.20.) Ford Box (Sunbeam No.8.) Ford & rear springs, pivot bolt, fitting new rear wing 3 pinion Fly car (Sunbeam M.9841. Div Train.) Sections Collecting, Evacuating, General Duty. B.Echelon N.T.A.S.C.	
"	28/1/16	Thurs.	WORKSHOP. Work on spring, hub cap & pinion (Sunbeam M.9841. Div Train.) Engine & brake (Ford No.20) Wheel & dynamo (Ford Seat). 2/LIEUT. B.E. SUTTON returned from Leave. Sections Collecting, Evacuating, General Duty.	
"	29/1/16	Fri.	WORKSHOP. Work on springs & pinion (Sunbeam M.9841. Div Train.) Footboard & saddle (Douglas b/cycle No.3 Sect.) Repairing Rotorby wheel & frame (No.3 Sect.) Staring & axle Rims & tock. Reported to D.D.S.T. & A.I.R.E. Sections Collecting, Evacuating, General duty. B.Echelon N.T.A.S.C.	
"	30/1/16	Sat.	WORKSHOP. Starting (Sunbeam M.9841. Div.Train.) Church Parade at 10.0.a.m. Sections Collecting, Evacuating.	
"	31/1/16	Sun.	WORKSHOP. Fitting new wing & shackle pins (Sunbeam M.9109. Div.Train.) Repairing springs (ALR.) Repairing tail (Sunbeam No.2). Repairing Rotorby bolt & pannier (No.3. Sect.) Despatch Ambulance at PHILOSOPHE. Sections Collecting, Evacuating, General duty. B.Echelon N.T.A.S.C.	

15th Bn Y.A.W.U.

Feb 1916

15th F.A.W.U.
vol: 8

Army Form C. 2118.

WAR DIARY
or
INTELLIGENCE SUMMARY.

(Erase heading not required.) 15th Divl Suppl M. Hackshaw Workshop Lieut RASC

Instructions regarding War Diaries and Intelligence Summaries are contained in F.S. Regs., Part II. and the Staff Manual respectively. Title pages will be prepared in manuscript.

Place	Date	Hour	Summary of Events and Information	Remarks and references to Appendices
MEUX-LES-MINES	1/2/16	Tues	WORKSHOP. Work on shackle pins & bushes fainting ear (Sunbeam N. 9209. 10th Divl Train) Repairing handle bars for tools (Rudge cycle No 2. Sect) Setting up & repairing Sunbeam front spring (Ltk). Section Collecting, Evacuating & general duties. B.E. Hutton Lieut RASC	
"	2/2/16	Wed	WORKSHOP. Setting front spring with new shackle pins & bushes & removing near shackle pins & painting car (Sunbeam N. 9209. Divl Train) Taking down tail tank & repairing un clips (Sunbeam N. 9811. Divl Train) Adjusting brakes & cover (Sunbeam N 9841. Divl Train) Repairing handlebars, footrests & seat (Rudge cycle No 2. sect). Section Collecting and Evacuating. B.E. Hutton Lt RASC	
"	3/2/16	Thurs	WORKSHOP. Repairing & refitting pedal tank (Sunbeam N. 9839 Divl Train) Repairing mudguards, side brake lever, & fitting fill wrench to rear axle (Ford No. 2.). Turning shackle pins & bushes & painting car (Sunbeam N. 9209. Divl Train). Section Collecting & Evacuating. B.E. Hutton Lt RASC	
"	4/2/16	Fri	WORKSHOP. Painting & various repairs carburetor inlet tube (Sunbeam N. 14482. Divl Train) Setting up & preparing spring (Ltk). Section Collecting, Evacuating.	
"	5/2/16	Sat	WORKSHOP. Repairing & painting car (Sunbeam N. 9209. Divl Train) Settling up & preparing spring (clutch) Setting up & fitting new wing (Sunbeam N. 9209. Divl Train). Painting car fitting new wing (Sunbeam N. 14482. Divl Train) took a Rudge cycle (No. 2 Sect). Section Collecting & Evacuating. B.E. Hutton Lt RASC	
"	6/2/16	Sun	WORKSHOP. Finishing & painting (Sunbeam N. 9209. Divl Train) Taking down gear box & dismantling same (Painter N 9245. Divl Sigl G.R.E.) B.E. Hutton Lt RASC	
"	7/2/16	Mon	WORKSHOP. Dismantling & examining gear box (Daimler M545. Sigl Co.) Refitting brake rod bands (Ford No. 14. km 2 Sect) Repairing silt tube level Ford No. 7. (No 1. Set) Section Collecting & Evacuating. B.E. Hutton Lt RASC	
"	8/2/16	Tues	WORKSHOP. Fitting new gear wheels & assembling box (Daimler M 545. Sigl Co) Nightering Ec. rod pin (No 18. lorry No. 3 Section). Repairing tail lamp	

1577 Wt W10791/1773 500,000 1/15 D.D.&L. A.D.S.S./Forms/C. 2118.

Army Form C. 2118.

WAR DIARY
or
INTELLIGENCE SUMMARY.

(Erase heading not required.) 15th Divl Sig. Co. Mechanical Transport Shops A.S.C. R.E.

Instructions regarding War Diaries and Intelligence Summaries are contained in F.S. Regs., Part II. and the Staff Manual respectively. Title pages will be prepared in manuscript.

Place	Date	Hour	Summary of Events and Information	Remarks and references to Appendices
NOEUX-LES-MINES	8/2/16	—	WORKSHOP (cont'd) & fitting new gland (6 cyl tractor lorry No.17. No.3 Sect.). Repairing side lamp (Sunbeam M9840. Dist. Train). Repairing wiring (Douglas m/cycle No.2 Sect.). No.20 Ford (No.3 sect.) Evacuated to 3rd M.T.A.C. Repair Shops, ST. OMER with faulty magneto ext. Section. Collecting & Evacuating.	B.E. Dutton M.T.A.S.C.
"	9/2/16	cont'd	WORKSHOP. Adjusting brakes (No.15 tractor lorry. No.3 Sect.). Assembling new big gear box (Daimler M.9.5. Signal Co.) Renewing shackle pins, facing & grinding in valves. (Sunbeam M.9840 Dist.Train.) Rebushing tie rod pins (tractor lorry No.16. No.3.Sect). Overhauling magneto (Douglas m/cycle No.2. Sect) Section. Collecting & Evacuating.	B.E. Dutton M.T.A.S.C.
"	10/2/16	Thurs	WORKSHOP. Adjusting gears & repairing horn (Daimler M.9.5. Sigl Co.) Rebushing tie rod pins (No.15 tractor lorry No.3. Sect). Steering grinding in valves & examining chassis (Sunbeam M.9840. Dist. Train.). Dist Train. Repairing poppet head & turning ordering piece (Workshop Lathe). Overhauling magneto (Douglas m/cycle No.2 Sect) Section. Collecting, Evacuating & general duty. B.E.Dutton M.T.A.S.C.	
"	11/2/16	Fri	WORKSHOP. Examining pump & grinding in valves & replacing hub cover distance piece. (Sunbeam M9840. Dist. Train). Straightening grand axle (Sunbeam No.5 No.1.Sect). Fitting and spring each side, new wind screen (Sunbeam M9240 Dist Train) Repairing side lamp (No.10 Wolseley), Spring Sunbeam, shackle pins (Stock). Repairing poppet head (Lathe).	B.E. Dutton M.T.A.S.C.
"	12/2/16	Sat	WORKSHOP. Fitting new spring, adjusting brakes & repairing the poppet head. Repairing & hand screen (Sunbeam M9840 Dist. Train.) Fitting wind screen (Sunbeam M9840 Dist Train). Section. Collecting & Evacuating.	B.E. Dutton M.T.A.S.C.
"	13/2/16	Sun	WORKSHOP. Fitting new spring & adjusting brakes (Sunbeam M9840. Dist.Train.) Repairing to the poppet head. Repairing & hand lifts B.S.A. m/cycle No.3 Section). Imported to D.D.S.T. 1st Army. Section. Collecting & Evacuating.	B.E. Dutton M.T.A.S.C.

Army Form C. 2118.

WAR DIARY
or
INTELLIGENCE SUMMARY.

(Erase heading not required.) 15th Div. Field Ambulance Workshop Unit ADC

Instructions regarding War Diaries and Intelligence Summaries are contained in F. S. Regs., Part II. and the Staff Manual respectively. Title pages will be prepared in manuscript.

Place	Date	Hour	Summary of Events and Information	Remarks and references to Appendices
NOEUX-LES-MINES	14/2/16	Mon	WORKSHOP Turning & fitting sliding tie rod bushes (Motor Amb.No 18 Mo3sect), Alteration to New Ford (No.20. No 3sect). Inspected ambulances at NOEUX-LES-MINES, PHILOSOPHE & MAZINGARBE. Section Collecting & Generally.	B Hutton Lt.RAMC
"	15/2/16	Tues	WORKSHOP Rebrazing steering tie rod (Ford (Motor Amb. No 17). Repairs to steering (3 ton Halfords lorry, 8th Co. R.E.- breakdown) Altering Body (Ford No 20) Repairing running board & wing (Sunbeam No.9) Section Collecting & Generally.	B Hutton Lt.RAMC
"	16/2/16	Wed.	WORKSHOP Taxing in cars & dismantling back axle (Vauxhall M9839, Dis.Train, turning shackle pins (VFA) & overhauling magneto (Daylee M.Cycle No. 2 Sect). Altering body (Ford No 20). Section Collecting & Generally	B Hutton Lt.RAMC
"	17/2/16	Thurs.	WORKSHOP Repairs to differential (Vauxhall 9839 Dist. train). Refitting front wheel to ball race & repairing suspension. (No 2. Sunbeam), turning & fitting new & old bushes (No.10 totally). Repairing side brake (Ford No.7). Repairing side brake (Ford No.7). Altering interior of body (Ford No 16 2d). Taxing Sunbeam shackle pins for Sunbeam. Section Collecting & Generally.	B Hutton Lt.RAMC
"	18/2/16	Fri	WORKSHOP. Repairing differential Sunbeam M9 839 Dist Train) Repairing Hub & &c, & fitting spring extension (No 2. Sunbeam). Refitting cam carrier & spring gear wheel carrier (Sunbeam 4482. Dist Train). Altering body (Ford No.20). Refitting & repairing Sunbeam M 9014 Dist Train, turning Sunbeam Shackle Pins for Stock. Section Collecting & Generally.	B Hutton Lt.RAMC
"	19/2/16	Sat.	WORKSHOP. Altering differential casing & driving shaft (Sunbeam M9839 Dist Train). Fitting new rear shackle pins (Sunbeam No 11) Repairing clutch (No. 6. Sunbeam). Altering exhaust pipe (No 15. totally) Altering body (No 20 Ford) Section Collecting & Generally. & repairs to 2nd Reporter. B Hutton Lt.RAMC	B Hutton Lt.RAMC
"	20/2/16	Sun	WORKSHOP Packing driving shaft, & fitting joint (Sunbeam M9014 2nd Train) Altering body (South 2nd Altering exhaust Pipe No 15 totally). Church Parade 10 a.m. Section Collecting & Generally	B Hutton Lt.RAMC

1577 Wt.W10791/1773 500,000 1/15 D.D. & L. A.D.S.S./Forms/C. 2118.

WAR DIARY
or
INTELLIGENCE SUMMARY.

Army Form C. 2118.

(Erase heading not required.) 15th Div. Suppl. Col. Mechanical Transport Coy A.S.C.

Instructions regarding War Diaries and Intelligence Summaries are contained in F.S. Regs., Part II and the Staff Manual respectively. Title pages will be prepared in manuscript.

Place	Date	Hour	Summary of Events and Information	Remarks and references to Appendices
NOEUX-LES-MINES	21/2/16	Mor.	WORKSHOP. Turning brake-second-being differential (Sunbeam M9834 Dist. Van.) Altering body (Ford No.20) Altering spring saddle pin (Ford No.20) Fitting exhaust pipe (Ford totally). Sections Collecting and Evacuating.	B.Sm. Tn. M.T.A.C.
"	22/2/16	Tues.	WORKSHOP. Assembling & fitting differential to Sunbeam M9834 Dist. Van. Fitting new spring central pin, adjusting & fitting & fitting tom belt. (No.4. Sunbeam) Altering body (Ford No.20). Sections Collecting, Evacuating & general duty.	B.Sm. Tn. M.T.A.C.
"	23/2/16	Wed.	WORKSHOP. Repairing petrol tank & Sunbeam M9834 Dist. Van. & Fitting new magneto switch. Pin A.S. Sunbeam Altering body (Ford No.20) 18 of fleet during night. Had all engines started up during night. Sections No.1&2 Evacuating, No.3 Collecting, Evacuating.	B.Sm. Tn. M.T.A.C.
"	24/2/16	Thurs.	WORKSHOP. Removing & fitting sorted Stoker-Squire Lorry M7194. Dis.Repd(6). Straightening & re-tooth overhauling casing (Ford No.21)Removing Thy Differential (Sunbeam No.2). Fixing a slipping forks for Bipods. Sections Collecting, Evacuating.	B.Sm. Tn. M.T.A.C.
"	25/2/16	Frid.	WORKSHOP. Dismantling Differential (No.2. Sunbeam) Cleaning offender deposit, inside & outside, cleaning sump, (Stoker-Squire Lorry M7194. Dis.Repd.(6) Placing clutch & tripod-forks. Sections Collecting, Evacuating.	B.Sm. Tn. M.T.A.C.
"	26/2/16	Sat.	WORKSHOP. Fitting & end tubing to differential casing, Fitting up near spring & Sunbeam, Straightening leaf, filling & inserting centre pin, reassembling spring. Cleaning cylinder, sump, & overhead & mapin (Stoker-Squire Lorry M7194. Dis.Repd.(6) Removing cylinder heads, fitting ones ends & connecting up one and out (Ford No.1) Fitting petrol can carrier Sunbeam M9041. Dist. Van.) Repairing radiator (Stoker-Squire Lorry 7194. Dis.Repd.(6.R.E.) Sections Collecting, Evacuating. Reported to D.D. of S.V. at R.A.R.E. Weekly Return form &c. Return introduced.	R.Sm. Tn. M.T.A.C.
"	27/2/16	Sun.	WORKSHOP. Assembling differential & attaching spring (Sunbeam M9034. Dist. Van.) Grinding cylinder, re-annealing crank	

1577 Wt. W10791/1773 500,000 1/15 D. D. & L. A.D.S.S./Forms/C. 2118.

Army Form C. 2118.

WAR DIARY
or
INTELLIGENCE SUMMARY.

(Erase heading not required.) 5th Dist Field Ambulance Workshop Unit ADC

Place	Date	Hour	Summary of Events and Information	Remarks and references to Appendices
MEUX-LES-MINES.	27/2/16	Sun.	WORKSHOP (contd) Sundry carbe for for truck spring (Sunbeam Squire Lorry 15th Div Signal Co.) Fitting 2 connecting rods & sundry engine's radiator (Ford No.Y) Repairing radiator, filling new fan belt (Sunbeam Squire Lorry 15th Div Signal Co.) Sunbury repairs for workshop. Ford Ambulance No.18605 (presented by the Boy Scouts Association transferred to 2nd Div F.A. No.2. Ford No.9708 received in exchange. Section Collecting Movements. B.R. Lister M.T.A.S.C.	
MEUX-LES-MINES.	28/2/16	Mon.	WORKSHOP Repairing mudguards, & body, taking of play in steering tie rod (Ford No.2.) Assembly engine, repairing radiator, fitting new sleeve to rear hub, turning eccentric. (Sunbeam Squire Lorry Bos Signal Co.) Overhauling steering (No.7 Ford). Fitting differential charging lubricating oil (No.2 Sunbeam) Section Collecting Movements. B.R. Lister M.T.A.S.C.	
MEUX-LES-MINES.	29/2/16	Tues.	WORKSHOP Repairing radiator, overhauling injectors (Ford No.7.) Removing engine from box from chassis (No.10 Hupmobile). Section Collecting Movements. B.R. Lister M.T.A.S.C. Adjusting heads (Ford No.7.) Removing engine from box from chassis (No.10 Hupmobile). Section Collecting Movements. B.R. Lister M.T.A.S.C.	

WAR DIARY OF

15th Divisional Field Ambulance - Workshop Unit A.S.C.

For the month of March 1916

COMMITTEE FOR THE
MEDICAL HISTORY OF THE WAR

Date   9- JUN.'16

15DW
F.A.W.U
Vol 9

WAR DIARY
INTELLIGENCE SUMMARY

Army Form C. 2118.

(Erase heading not required.) 15th Div: Field Amb Lorry workshop Unit A.S.C.

Instructions regarding War Diaries and Intelligence Summaries are contained in F.S. Regs., Part II. and the Staff Manual respectively. Title pages will be prepared in manuscript.

Place	Date	Hour	Summary of Events and Information	Remarks and references to Appendices
NOEUX-LES-MINES	1/3/16	Wed.	WORKSHOP. Work on Steering (Stacker Lyine Lorry Siphal 6.), Gear Box & Steering (Hupmobile No.10). Steering (Ford No.14). Exhaust box (Ford No.6). Front wheel ball race (Sunbeam M/4488. Divisional). Refye/ld (No 2 Last) Springs (Ford) for stock. Section Collecting & evacuating from PHILOSOPHE, MAZINGARBE & LOOS. Inspected ambulance staff Sergt CUTLER. B.Shelton W.H.A.C.	
"	2/3/16	Thurs.	WORKSHOP. Work on brakes (Stacker-Lyine Lorry Siphal 6.), Gear Box & Universal joints (Hupmobile No.10) Steering Collecting & evacuating from PHILOSOPHE, MAZINGARBE, LOOS to NOEUX-LES-MINES. B.Shelton W.H.A.C.	
"	3/3/16	Frid.	WORKSHOP. Assembling gear box (Hupmobile No.10). Overhauling (Austin workshop Engine) Section Collecting & evacuating from PHILOSOPHE, MAZINGARBE, LOOS. B.Shelton W.H.A.C.	
"	4/3/16	Sat.	WORKSHOP. Overhauling Engine (Sunbeam M.T. 14482. Div.Train.) Erecting gear box & work on searching (Hupmobile No.10) Section Collecting & evacuating from PHILOSOPHE, MAZINGARBE & LOOS. Inspected to D.D.G.V.S. at SAREE. B.Shelton W.H.A.C.	
"	5/3/16	Sun.	WORKSHOP. Assembling Engine, tightening compartits, testing (Hupmobile No.10). Repairing mudguards etc (Sunbeam No.11) Section Collecting & evacuating from PHILOSOPHE, MAZINGARBE & LOOS. B.Shelton W.H.A.C.	
"	6/3/16	Mon.	WORKSHOP. Returning stocks of Stores div inspt. Section Collecting and evacuating at adv. Dressing Station. B.Shelton W.H.A.C.	
"	7/3/16	Tues.	WORKSHOP. Overhauling Engine (Ridge & Peele No 2 Bet). Testing Sunbeam Shaft & rims 10 set Try up Road Springs (Stock) Section Collecting & evacuating from MAZINGARBE, PHILOSOPHE & LOOS. B.Shelton W.H.A.C.	
"	8/3/16	Wed.	WORKSHOP. Overhauling Engine (Sunbeam M 9840. Div Train), Vilifying float shell ballrace & repairing dust cap (Ch.R. Sunbeam). Turning limbers shackle pins (stock). Inspected ambulances at MAZINGARBE, PHILOSOPHE, NOEUX-LES-MINES A.M. Staff Sergt CUTLER. Section Collecting & evacuating. B.Shelton W.H.A.C.	

WAR DIARY
or
INTELLIGENCE SUMMARY.

Army Form C. 2118.

(Erase heading not required.) 15th Dist. M.M. Ambulance Workshop Unit. M.T.A.S.C.

Instructions regarding War Diaries and Intelligence Summaries are contained in F. S. Regs., Part II. and the Staff Manual respectively. Title pages will be prepared in manuscript.

Place	Date	Hour	Summary of Events and Information	Remarks and references to Appendices
NOEUX-LES-MINES.	9/3/16	Thurs.	WORKSHOP. Repairing Springs (Sunbeam No.9840 Dist train.) Overhauling springs & trucks (No.8 Sunbeam) Repairing workshop stops. Sections collecting & overhauling.	B&W.Tr. M.T.A.S.C.
NOEUX-LES-MINES.	10/3/16	Frid.	WORKSHOP. Work on springs (Sunbeams Nos.1, 2 & 3, M.T. 9840) & Clutch (Sunbeam No.8) Altering body (Ford No.14) Sections Collecting & overhauling from LOOS, PHILOSOPHE & MAZINGARBE.	B&W.Tr. M.T.A.S.C.
NOEUX-LES-MINES.	11/3/16	Sat.	WORKSHOP. Adjusting Clutch (Sunbeam M.T.9840) Smoke springs (Sunbeam No.2) Altering Body overhauling Steering (Ford No.21) Sections Collecting & overhauling from LOOS, PHILOSOPHE & MAZINGARBE. Reported to D.D. of S.&T. First Army at H.R.E.	B&W.Tr. M.T.A.S.C.
NOEUX-LES-MINES.	12/3/16	Sun.	WORKSHOP. Overhauling differential & gearbox. (Daimler M.T.395 Signal Co.) Altering body & overhauling Steering (Ford No.14). Lightning lamp rod & fairing wheel Spanners (workshops) Sections Collecting & overhauling from Nos Branch. Section B&W.Tr. M.T.A.S.C. (Lorries No.18). Work on brakes (Ford No.21) Stairs (Sunbeam No.12)	B&W.Tr. M.T.A.S.C.
NOEUX-LES-MINES.	13/3/16	Mon.	WORKSHOP. Work on differential & gearbox (Daimler No.395. Signal Co.) Springs & altering (Sunbeam No.12). Steering & body alteration (Ford No.14) Repairing wheel spanners (workshops) Sections Collecting & overhauling	B&W.Tr. M.T.A.S.C.
NOEUX-LES-MINES.	14/3/16	Tues.	WORKSHOP. Work on gear box. (Daimler M.T.395. Signal Co.) Body (Ford No.14) Springs (Sunbeam No.12) Steering & tyres rod (workshops No.18). Stationary Engine (Signal Co.) Overhauling & workshop Dynamo. Sections Collecting & overhauling.	B&W.Tr. M.T.A.S.C.
NOEUX-LES-MINES.	15/3/16	Wed.	WORKSHOP. Assembling gear box & differential (Daimler M.T.395. Signal Co.) Altering body (Ford No.14) Work on Springs (Sunbeam No.12). Lifting today & fixing (Signal Co.) Overhauling Stationary Engine (Signal Co.) Verify double pins for stock. Re sheets of ambulances of Rds. Besides Stations with Staff Surg. CUTLER. Sections Collecting & overhauling.	B&W.Tr. M.T.A.S.C.
NOEUX-LES-MINES	16/3/16	Thurs.	WORKSHOP. Work on Stationary Engine (Signal Co.) Altering body & Springs (Ford No.14). Lamp bracket (Workshop cycle) Spring for stock. Sections Collecting & overhauling.	B&W.Tr. M.T.A.S.C.

1577 Wt. W10791/1773 500,000 7/15 D. D. & L. A.D.S.S./Forms/C. 2118.

WAR DIARY
INTELLIGENCE SUMMARY

Army Form C. 2118.

15th Divl. Sup. Column, Ambulance Workshop Unit, A.S.C.

Place	Date	Hour	Summary of Events and Information	Remarks and references to Appendices
NOEUX-LES-MINES	17/3/16	Fri.	WORKSHOP. Assembling rebuilt Stationary Engine (Signal Co.) Repairs to hub caps, door lock (Sunbeam No.4.) Repairs to springs (Sunbeam No.3. & Sunbeam M/C 9840 Div. Train.) Fitting turning transplates for universal joint cover (Sunbeam No.12.) Repairs to head lamps (Wolseley No.10.) Setting up Sunbeam springs for stock. Section Collecting & General fty. No.1. 372 mls. No.2. 74 mls. No.3. 31 mls. B.B.Dutton Lt. A.S.C.	
NOEUX-LES-MINES	18/3/16	Sat.	WORKSHOP. Repairs to Springs (Sunbeams Nos.1, 8 & Stock). Repairs to hand Lifts (B.S.A. m/cycle). Repairs to Brake (Sunbeam No.2.) Alterations to body (Ford No.14.) Section Collecting & General fty. No.1. 280 mls. No.2. 322 mls. No.3. 60 mls. Inspected B.D.D.G.T.N. at M.T.R.E. B.B.Dutton Lt. A.S.C.	
NOEUX-LES-MINES	19/3/16	Sun.	WORKSHOP. Painting body (Ford No.14.) Fitting spring centre pin (Wolseley No.16.) Repairs to Spring (Sunbeam No.16.) Overhauling steering, adjusting bands (Ford No.2D.) Fitting fan belts & repairing springs (Sunbeam No.1.) Section Collecting & General fty. No.1. 330 mls. No.2. 120 mls. No.3. 21 mls. B.B.Dutton Lt. A.S.C.	
NOEUX-LES-MINES	20/3/16	Mon.	WORKSHOP. Work on front axle ball race & springs (Sunbeam M.T.9209. Div. Train.) Work on springs of Sunbeam M.T.9839. Div. Train. & Fords Nos.1 & 2. Side trapper cover altered & adjustment. (Daimler M.T.395 Signal Co.) Painting car (Ford No.14.) Forging Sunbeam Shackle pins & setting up springs for stock. Section Collecting & General fty. No.1. 92 mls, No.2. 161 mls, No.3. 34 mls. B.B.Dutton Lt. A.S.C.	
NOEUX-LES-MINES	21/3/16	Tues.	WORKSHOP. Overhauling Springs (Sunbeam M.9839. Div. Train Pk.1.) Overhauling Steering (Sunbeam M.9209. Div. Train.) Buffers exhaust pipe & stop iron. (Wolseley No.15.) Fitting Brackets & Tarpaulin hinges for Stretcher racks (Sunbeam No.1.) Setting up & fitting Sunbeam Springs for stock. Section Collecting & General fty. No.1. 202 mls, No.2. 160 mls, No.3. 106 mls. B.B.Dutton Lt. A.S.C.	
MOEUX-LES-MINES	22/3/16	Wed.	WORKSHOP. Took on Steering repairs (Sunbeam M.9209. Div. Train.) Rear Brake (Sunbeam No.1.) Spring (Sunbeam No.1.) Radiator (Wolseley M.595 Signal Co.) Caulking tea boilers, removing Exhaust pipe (John Stream Disinfector) Section No.1. 283 mls, No.2. Q.G. 2nd s No.3. 102 mls. B.B.Dutton Lt. A.S.C.	

WAR DIARY
INTELLIGENCE SUMMARY

Army Form C. 2118.

Place	Date	Hour	Summary of Events and Information	Remarks and references to Appendices
NOEUX-LES-MINES	23/3/16	Thurs.	WORKSHOP. Took on Steering (Sunbeam No 9209. Div. Train). Reptd. in. Staff H. today No. 16. Differential (Sunbeam No 214). Radiator (Daimler No 9195 Div Signal Co.) Side brake (Sunbeam No 12). Repairing 10 cwt. Pulley tubes (workshop). Section No. 1. Collecting Evacuating. No. 1. 97 m/s; No. 2. 64 m/s; No. 3. 137 m/s.	B. Hutton. It. A.S.C.
NOEUX-LES-MINES	24/3/16	Frid.	WORKSHOP. Took on Brakes, Hood (Sunbeam No 9839 Div. Train) Differential and Evacuating No. 1. 169 m/s; No. 2. 100 m/s; No. 3. 223 m/s.	B. Hutton. It. A.S.C.
NOEUX-LES-MINES	25/3/16	Sat.	WORKSHOP. Took on Springs, tie. bolts. (Sunbeam No 5, Ford No. 6). Repairing tot. tension. Sunbeam. tie. beam. No. 17063 (No. 2.) Staring to Col. to for Evacuation to 3rd MAC. Repairs photos. M. war. axle box k.c. Vacat. Went to LILLERS to find billets Wc. Section. Collectly. Evacuating. No. 1. 194 m/s; No. 2. 106 m/s; No. 3. 137 m/s	B. Hutton. It. A.S.C.
NOEUX-LES-MINES	26/3/16	Sun.	WORKSHOP Valuing Stores to LILLERS. Jarringed billets LILLERS. Section. Collectly. Evacuating. No. 1. 189 m/s; No. 2. Nil. No. 3. 144 m/s	B. Hutton. It. A.S.C.
LILLERS.	27/3/16	Mon.	WORKSHOP. Moved from NOEUX-LES-MINES to LILLERS. Section. Collectly. Evacuating. No. 1. 199 m/s; No. 2. 80 m/s; No. 3. 128 m/s. Rolled Lorry No. R. 15511 received from Army Lorries (dift) Chain breakage under No. 15063	B. Hutton. It. A.S.C.
LILLERS.	28/3/16	Tues.	WORKSHOP. Repairing cancrof. Lorry (Peerless M.T) (Reblt by Dray No. 2.) took on retd. unrepaired tracks (worksp.) Storing (workshop. (lorry). Section. Collectly. Evacuating. No. 1. 8 m/s; No. 2. 168 m/s; No. 3. 57 m/s.	B. Hutton. It. A.S.C.
LILLERS.	29/3/16	Wed.	WORKSHOP. Took on footbrak. Spring, tank fitting, Radiator. (Ford No. 21.) Took on Head Lamp for war. Spring. Sunbeam No. 9846. Div. Train.) Alterig top Gate. (Ford No. F) filling to tally arranged (workshp. Dray. No. 2.) Section No. 1. 64 m/s; No. 2. 38 m/s; No. 3. 50 m/s	B. Hutton. It. A.S.C.

Army Form C. 2118.

WAR DIARY
or
INTELLIGENCE SUMMARY.

(Erase heading not required.) 3rd Dist. Field Ambulance Workshop Unit ADS

Instructions regarding War Diaries and Intelligence Summaries are contained in F. S. Regs., Part II. and the Staff Manual respectively. Title pages will be prepared in manuscript.

Place	Date	Hour	Summary of Events and Information	Remarks and references to Appendices
LILLERS.	30/3/16	Thurs	WORKSHOP. Took a clutch painting. (Sunbeam No.8) Springs, clutch, gear box & fan belt. (Sunbeam M9841. Dist Train.) Knock axle (Sunbeam M9839. Dist Train.) Mudguard & seat at 2 9.O.C. Lorry) Altering Body (Ford No.7.) Sections collecting & generally general duty. No.1. 102 miles; No.2. 18 mls; No.3. 119 miles. B.B. Ltn. ST H.A.C.	
LILLERS.	31/3/16	Frid.	WORKSHOP. Work on springs (Sunbeam No.3.) Rewire paddle, stard and radius rod (Ford No.14.) Differential springs (Sunbeam M9839. Dist Train) Altering body & making seats (Ford No.7.) Repairing tool box etc (Sunbeam No.12.) Sections collecting & generally. No.1. 38 miles; No.2. 111 miles; No.3. 67 mls. B.B. Ltn. ST H.A.C.	

1577 Wt. W10791/1773 500,000 1/15 D. D. & L. A.D.S.S./Forms/C. 2118.

www.ingramcontent.com/pod-product-compliance
Lightning Source LLC
Chambersburg PA
CBHW081425160426
43193CB00013B/2194